# JOHN ELIOT
## "APOSTLE TO THE INDIANS"

# JOHN ELIOT

## "APOSTLE TO THE INDIANS"

By

### OLA ELIZABETH WINSLOW

ILLUSTRATED WITH PHOTOGRAPHS

*BOSTON*

HOUGHTON MIFFLIN COMPANY

1 9 6 8

"THE WORLD IS BETTER ABLE TO READ
THE NATURE OF RELIGION IN A MAN'S
LIFE THAN IN THE BIBLE."

*Richard Baxter*

## TABLE OF
## CONTENTS

## LIST OF
## ILLUSTRATIONS

FOLLOWING PAGE 116

# JOHN ELIOT
## "APOSTLE TO THE INDIANS"

## INTRODUCTION

AMONG THE STALWART ONES of New England's first generation, John Eliot holds his place in the small group of
men who wrote their names indelibly on the first pages of our
national history. Pioneers are not always men of the gentler
virtues, but John Eliot was one of the gentlest of men and
beloved by hundreds, as such men deserve to be. He was also
a man of superb courage. Faced on one occasion by an angry
sagamore with a knife in his hand, he could say, "I am about
the work of the great God, and he is with me, so that I fear
not all the sachems of the country. I'll go on, and do you
touch me if you dare." [1] Soldierly words they are, and such
came naturally to John Eliot.

His own day called him "Apostle to the Indians," words
which still identify him to later generations, as a portrait
might, were we fortunate enough to have one. The portrait
that would represent him best would not show him in ministerial robes with velvet draperies behind him. Rather he
would be wearing a leathern coat and breeches and would be
standing, Bible in hand, in a forest clearing. A half circle of
Indian tepees against dark trees would be the background and
before him, squatted on the ground, would be a huddle of
blanketed Indians, their faces uplifted as they listened.

Unfortunately, most of his spoken words, as well as his fea-
tures, are lost to us. We have many letters reporting details of
his daily life, chiefly his work among the Indians. We have
also his translations, most notably that of the entire Bible into

the language of the Algonquians, or Massachusetts Indians. No man living now reads the Bible in this tongue. The Massachusetts Indians have almost disappeared. The Praying Towns John Eliot established, fourteen of them, have taken other names and their beginnings are almost forgotten.

It would not seem important to John Eliot that what modern times regard as his most significant legacy, his translation of the Bible, achieved by candlelight through many years, is now one of the most valuable early books America can claim. Although not exactly rare, at auctions it brings thousands. At the sale of May 6, 1966, a copy was purchased for $43,000, the second largest price ever paid for an American book. John Eliot had persevered in his effort to translate and print it for quite other reasons than fame or money. Personal ambition he did not know. His concern was with the souls of the Indians, lost souls as he thought, and the Bible would open a path to their salvation as he understood it. They must have this great book in their own tongue, and when it was in their hands, they must be taught to read it for themselves. Only then might they begin to understand that they had a share in God's plan for the whole human race.

He knew the magnitude of his self-appointed task. The Algonquian language had no written texts, no grammar, no dictionary, and only a scant vocabulary of spiritual experience. Not at all daunted, at forty-five he took the first step. Since there was no grammar, he would make one, and in this spirit he persevered until his translation of the entire Bible was behind him. Perhaps this is not the most important service he rendered, but there it is, to the wonder and admiration of linguistic scholars ever since.

Unlike a great humanitarian of our later day, he believed that civilization must go along with the religious services he offered. Dr. Albert Schweitzer is reported as saying to his critics, "I did not come here to civilize, but to heal." Perhaps civilization works best unheralded. Perhaps both men were saying (and doing) exactly the same thing, only with John Eliot, "civility," as he always called it, was a declared purpose.

His missionary labors are a noble story, spelled out through more than a half century of unceasing rigors which make the lives of his pulpit brethren in seventeenth-century towns appear almost comfortable. He had a fifty-eight-year pastorship in Roxbury, too, and was seldom absent on preaching days. But between one Sunday and the next, for more than forty years, he spent unnumbered days traveling the forest trails, fording unbridged rivers, his nightly shelter often only a blanket, his food carried in his pocket, as he journeyed once a fortnight to the scattered Indian villages, thirty, forty, even sixty and seventy miles from his Roxbury home.

"I have not been dry, night or day, from the third day of the week to the sixth," he once wrote in a rainy time, "but so travelled, and at night pull off my boots, wring my stockings, and on with them again. But God steps in and helps." [2] For John Eliot that made all the difference.

History is events, of course: discoveries, wars, treaties, constitutions, assemblies, schools, inventions, markets. But history is primarily people, their thoughts, their purposes, their convictions, their daily lives and how they lived them. John Eliot is one whose clear purpose and indefatigible labors, carried out no matter what the cost, have meaning for more than his own generation. He lived longer than most men who came in the first ships, and before he died in 1690, he had helped to plant certain stones that are deeply built into the foundations of American thought and concern far more than religion as he preached it.

Three hundred years erase much from a nation's memory, overlay much, destroy much, but something intangible remains even when the visible stones have crumbled. Something these first men carved into the thought and life of their time (so different from our own) still takes new forms of expression with every passing decade. Some of this may be found in the annual record of congressional action in Washington, D.C. The unrecorded part may be even more significant.

Posterity owes these first men more than the memory of their names. We owe them such understanding in the light of their own day as may still be recovered. The recall of John Eliot humbles us as we see the crystal clarity of his purpose, the steel of his endurance, the confidence of his far vision. He is part of the great spiritual tradition which dignifies our beginnings as a nation.

## TWENTY-SEVEN
## ENGLISH YEARS

JOHN ELIOT was twenty-seven years old when he boarded the good ship *Lyon* for Boston in 1631. Twenty-seven years are long enough for many things to be determined for the years that will follow. They are also too short a time for an earlier heritage to be established beyond change. Fifty-nine more years John Eliot would live, all of them in New England. He would not sail the ocean again. America would claim him and posterity would call him one of the founders. Inevitably, through these fifty-nine remaining years, as he became one of the leaders of first-generation settlers, what he had brought with him and what maturity would make of it would be built into the structure, the ideals, the future of the new nation.

Behind him lay an English heritage, personal and national, an English university education, commitment to a religious purpose that was just emerging in England and was hardly yet clarified. Young men of high thinking were being caught by it, particularly those who had been exposed to the influence of Cambridge University. Had John Eliot been ten years younger at the time of his decision to sail, the mere adventure of a vast new continent might have been a sufficient challenge for the risk involved, but by his twenty-seventh birthday, he had already gone far enough in his own thinking to bring to the experience just ahead of him a firm decision and a settled purpose. Both would be subject to change at that age, perhaps creative change.

His English heritage was in no way extraordinary. He was
the son of Bennett Eliot, an extensive landholder in Hertfordshire and Essex who called himself "yeoman." For his
day his holdings were above average for a man of his social
rank. We know his dates, his residence, his properties and the
names of his children in his will, but little else. The baptismal entry of his son John is preserved on the parish register of
the church of St. John the Baptist in Widford, a small village
on the river Lea, twenty-five miles from London. The record
reads, "Anno dm. John Elliott the sonne of Bennett Elliott
was baptized the fifte daye of August in the year of our Lord
1604." [1] Since baptism was usually less than a week after the
birth of a child, this entry probably establishes John Eliot's
birthday as of an early day in August of this year 1604.

The marriage entry of his parents is recorded in the same
parish. That record reads, "An° Dm. Bennett Eliot and Lettese Aggar were married the xxxth of October an° Sup.
Dicto." [2]

John was the third child of this marriage. The christening
of a sister Sarah, January 13, 1599/60, and a brother Philip,
April 25, 1602, are recorded in the same register. Both came
to New England shortly after John. A younger brother,
Jacob, baptized September 21, 1606, came later.

Fittingly, a memorial window to John Eliot was placed in
this church by American descendants on May 21, 1894. The
honor had been long postponed, because of uncertainty as to
his birthplace, until the discovery of his baptismal record in
Widford. On this date, a large congregation assembled,
including many from neighboring parishes. The United
States Ambassador, the Honorable T. F. Bayard, with his wife
and daughters, came from London, Mr. and Mrs. Curtis, rep-
resenting the descendants, from Boston. Reverend J. T.
Lockwood, rector of the church, gave a sketch of John Eliot's

life and work. A telegram from Roxbury church was read, "We honor the memory of our Apostle and try to carry on his work."

When the window was unveiled, Ambassador Bayard responded to the toast offered by the pastor of the church "to the United States of America and Great Britain," by saying, in conclusion, "I bow my head in admiration of John Eliot the English Apostle to what is now the United States of America." [3] A tablet in this church records those who have ministered here since the eleventh century. The nineteenth-century honor to John Eliot continues a noble story.

The village of Widford was also the home of other Eliots during the early years of the century. Children of William, Austen and Edward Eliot were baptized in the church of St. John the Baptist, Austen and George Eliot were married and Austen Eliot was buried here. Among other Eliots listed in the registers of the neighboring parishes of Waltham Abbey, Cheshunt, Hunsdon and Stortford of Hertfordshire and in various border villages of Essex, some may have been related to Bennett Eliot, but if so, those connections have not been established.[4] A persistent tradition attempts to tie the New England John Eliot with the Eliots whose pedigree is given in the *Visitations of Essex*. Various members of this family owned land in Widford and neighboring villages, but certain proof of this relationship is lacking. Also, the assumption of a connection between the New England John Eliot and Sir John Eliot of Cornwall, born in 1592 and parliamentary leader under Charles II, would seem to be entirely without foundation.

A somewhat vaguer tradition traces all the English Eliots to a knight, William d'Aliot, who came into England with William the Conqueror in 1066, but there is no known connection between the family of Bennett Eliot and any branch of that Eliot family.[5] One such branch includes the Eliots of East Coker, Somersetshire, from whom Charles W. Eliot, former President of Harvard, traced his line. Other Eliots in still earlier New England had come from other counties of the old country, for by the date of John Eliot's birth many English families bore the name. So far as has been certainly proved, however, his line can boast no illustrious forebear.

After 1610, four years from the christening in Widford of Jacob, John Eliot's younger brother, the baptisms of Bennett and Lettese Eliot's younger children are recorded in the church of Nazeing in Essex, just across the border from Hertfordshire. Three children were born here, Lydia, Francis and Mary, mentioned by Bennett Eliot in his will as "my youngest children." Lettese Eliot, wife and mother, lived only five days after the baptism of Mary, her seventh child. She was buried in Nazeing, March 16, 1620, and her husband, Bennett, a year and a half later, November 21, 1621.[6] At that time, John Eliot was in the university.

Widford, his birthplace, and Nazeing, his childhood home, have been touched lightly by the changes of time, although both are probably larger now than in John's day. Centuries earlier, this corner of England had been the theater of stormy events, chiefly great wars. Thousands had perished by the sword in these now quiet fields and pastures. Armies had marched, chariots had rolled along on these ancient roads in the conquests of Rome and the long wars of Saxon and Dane. Boadicea, Amazon queen of the Iceni, in her revolt against Rome, 61 A.D., had led her army along the river Lea against an even larger army of her enemy. Passionate and powerful she was, terrifying of aspect, harsh of voice and before her "murdering Charms whole Legions fell."

Many centuries later, King Alfred the Great dispersed the Danes and brought peace to his West Saxon kingdom in this neighborhood, and, finally, William the Conqueror crossed the Thames at Wallingford, burning and plundering as he came. Revolutions, persecutions and martyrdoms belonging to this region fill many pages of English history before the royal visitations of Queen Elizabeth tell a brighter story. She had spent much time here. After her death in 1603, the year before John Eliot's birth, a new Hertfordshire and Essex chapter began in which the boy would have scant share. The earlier story made the hero tales of his childhood which were doubtless remembered for life and probably told to his own children in far-off New England.

Today's visitor to Nazeing may still see the road from Waltham Abbey over which the legions marched. From the tower of the ivy-covered church, which stands on a slight eminence, Epping Forest is still visible far away. Closer at hand is the bare plain on which Queen Boadicea, a spear in her hand, her jewels glittering, defeated the Roman army. Inside the church one finds the oaken seats of the Eliot, Curtis, Ruggles, Heath, Graves, Peacock, Payson and other families from which young men set forth to New England.

John Eliot's childhood memories would have centered in this quiet village of Nazeing, but this story like that of the still earlier Widford, is a blank. In almost his only reference to his childhood, he paid tribute to the piety of his parents in these words, "I do see that it was a great favour of God unto me, to season my first times with the fear of God, the word, and prayer." [7]

Not surprising in this time and place. Christianity had taken a firm hold in Hertfordshire and Essex from Roman times on, and to some extent the traditions of this early faith had persisted through the centuries. Early martyrdoms by which priest and layman had paid the price of belief at the stake were still remembered when the Marian persecutions were in full storm. In their later day the protesting Lollards had been welcomed, and still later the migrating French Huguenots had found harbor here. Hospitality to Nonconformity had grown stronger with each succeeding generation, and it is not strange that in John Eliot's time Essex was one of the counties from which Nonconforming preachers, fleeing the strictures of Archbishop Laud, escaped to Holland and New England in full numbers. The list is long in American memory and many names on it are familiar. John Eliot was one of this number.

One approaches his life story, not only that of his childhood and of his decision as a young man to emigrate, but also that of his entire life, with the recognition that the turmoils of his day were religious. More properly, they were theological. Theology, during his generation, was not a strange subject, dark to all but the minister in his study. Its terminology was familiar both to the master and his apprentice and to children not yet in their teens. The political unrest already stirring in the first decades of the century had theological justification. Politics and theology were not in separate compartments. Safety both for the individual and the state lay in strict orthodoxy, and an uneducated laboring man, whether he was a professed Christian or not, had some notion as to what constituted safe orthodoxy. The seventeenth century in England was a theological age in direction and intensity of conviction to a degree greater than any other century before or since. Religion both for the common man and the man of great intellectual gifts could lead to such a passionate absorption and such completeness of surrender as to produce some of the saintliest men who have ever lived — Richard Baxter, for example. It also led other men, and among them some of the most gifted, to extravagance and childish credulity. Paradox is part of the picture. To understand this age politically, socially, secularly, as well as religiously, one must begin with the dominance of theology in the thinking of all men and also be aware that it could lead them in diametrically opposed directions.

The religious views which Englishmen of high and low degree took for granted in their thought of themselves, their sovereign, her government and their responsibilities as citizens as well as church members, can be found in contemporary publications of all sorts: in sermons, of course, particularly those preached before Parliament; in controversial pamphlets, both political and religious; royal proclamations; popular broadsides; and perhaps most plainly of all, in manuals of devotion, more popular then than any other books. One such publicaton, layman John Norden's *A Progress of Piety*, was first printed in 1591 and again in 1596. It was dedicated to Queen Elizabeth, "Servant of the Great King," as the author's *Mirrour for the Multitude* had been, five years earlier. In the phrases of his "Motion of a Prayer" for her, she had been "chosen by the Lord himself," and because of her England now had "the freedom and Liberty of the Gospel" which "before her days was stopt up with the briars and thorns of persecution and death," but is now "laid open again." She leads us "by her sacred government through the wilderness of all the divisions, hurlyburlies, and tumults in the world." The favor of God is upon her, and "all the nations of the world do see and consider that great is her God." [8]

A book such as this was often the only volume aside from the Bible in middle-class homes of the English villages. It was intended "for us who are the common people," and its influence was past calculation. John Norden's *The Pensive Man's Practice*, first printed in 1585, had gone through forty editions. Books of prayer mainly, these volumes cover almost the

entire range of human need which religion can satisfy: confession of sin, unworthiness and weakness, pleas for strength
and protection, praise and adoration of God, thanksgiving.
For those who are inarticulate, these prayers, brief and in
simple language, enlarge a devout man's capacity, both for a
sense of need and a path toward its fulfillment.

Such prayers and other encouragements to piety as fill the
pages of these manuals were part of the "household religion"
enjoined in a marginal gloss to the story of Abraham (Genesis
17:23) in the Geneva Bible. "Masters in their houses," it
read, "ought to be as preachers to their families," and so it
was. Devotional writers put the phrase "household religion"
in their titles and presented it on page after page until it was
not only a current phrase all over England but was also prac-
ticed with daily religious exercises.

"If ever we would have the church of God to continue
among us, we must bring it into our households, and nourish
it in our families," [9] wrote Richard Greenham, and his counsel was echoed by other writers and observed by devout masters of families.

A long tradition also upheld this duty, emphasized as it had
been by Luther, Calvin and Tyndale. If the clergy were cor-
rupt, the soundness of family orthodoxy would protect the
new generation. Authority was in the father's hand, effective
not only for his children, but also for the apprentices who
were often members of his household. The family as a unit
was recognized by heads of government as responsible for
teaching children the essentials of devotion and guiding them
in the practice of piety as well as enforcing law and order
within the home circle. John Eliot's tribute to his home
training could have been echoed in hundreds of homes
throughout England in the first decade of the new century.
Such early training was for him the first chapter in his long
story.

School life also had a religious tone from the days of the hornbook through the university. The Bible, prayer and orthodox doctrine were a large part of the content of education, and devotional exercises belonged to every day's routine from a child's earliest years. The *ABC* was the first book put into his hands. Issued by royal authority, it cost one penny in paper, two pennies in parchment. It contained the alphabet, numbers from one to three hundred, the Lord's Prayer and such elementary religious material as was thought necessary for a child to know. After Queen Elizabeth came to the throne, this first book was usually combined with the *Syllabarium,* beginning with ab, eb, ib, ub, etc., and ending with the phrase, "In the name of the Father, of the Son, and of the Holy Ghost." The catechism and the graces before and after meat followed, one of them ending, "God save his church, our Queen and Realm, and send us Peace in Christ our Lord, Amen." At the close of this little volume was the quatrain:

> This little Catechism learned
> by Heart (for so it ought)
> The Primer next commanded
> is for Children to be taught.[10]

In a pious home, such as John Eliot's tribute to his parents suggests, both the *ABC* and the *Primer* were probably taught by his father. If not, the dame school of the village would have taken his place.

Aged six or seven, with elementary reading, writing and figuring begun, John would have been ready for grammar school. In his county of Essex, even fifty years before his birth, there had been seventeen grammar schools, and it is likely that his own village of Nazeing provided one when he was ready for it. His grammar school training, whether he received it here or in a neighboring village, apparently proceeded smoothly, for he was enrolled as a pensioner in Jesus

College, Cambridge University, during the Lenten term, 1618, several months before his fourteenth birthday. Behind him now were some seven years of training in Latin, both read and spoken, probably also some Greek and Hebrew, acquaintance with the Bible, both text and history, the beginning of logic, training in public speaking and the writing of Latin verses.

By choosing Cambridge instead of Oxford he had put himself directly in touch with the specific religious influences that in a few more years would bring him to New England. In 1618, when he entered, the university numbered nearly three thousand students, large enough to seem almost a world to a village boy. Jesus College, in numbers one of the smallest units of the university was far removed from the town, surrounded by open fields and groves. Its enrollment would even decrease during John Eliot's residence, for this was the time of Roger Andrewes as master, and his personal supervision of the college was very slight. He was a scholar of ability and had been one of the translators of the King James Bible, but college teaching and administration were not among his interests. He came in 1618, the year of John Eliot's admission, and remained until 1632 when, after a year's absence, complaints against him had so increased that he surrendered his mastership. Possibly respect for his more famous brother, Lancelot Andrewes, had protected him from an earlier dismissal.

John Eliot did not experience the new spirit of the college which came about after his departure as students began to increase and the college to enjoy better days. For him Jesus College had been a quiet harbor, well deserving of King James' remark on one of his visits to the university. "Most collegiate," he had said, "retired from the town in a meditative posture, alone by itself."

Originally the seat of a Benedictine nunnery, it had always

been a quiet harbor. Probably founded in 1133, dedicated to St. Radegund and under the patronage of the bishops of Ely, its detailed early history is somewhat shadowy. Generations of devout nuns had lived here performing their services of hospitality to travelers, being charitable to the poor of the neighborhood, directing the farmers who plowed and sowed the nunnery's extensive acres and managing a company of household workers who brewed ale, made candles, wove cloth and carried on the annual fair at the Feast of the Assumption. Ill fortune came. In 1277 the bell tower fell; in 1313 and 1375 destructive fires followed; in 1390 a furious gale brought heavy damage; but even so the busy life went on after each disaster. After some three centuries poverty proved too formidable and corruption set in. Debt and scandal entered the story. Fields were left unplowed, the beautiful buildings fell into disrepair, several nuns cast off the veil and those who were left entered other religious houses.

In 1497 the nunnery was chartered as a college, its existing buildings were repaired and slowly adapted to student use.[11] In spite of outward changes, however, the monastic character of the establishment remains to this day. Its cloistered quadrangle has no counterpart in the university. Its gateway tower leads into a court open to the fields on one side. The stone bench, where on Maundy Thursday the twelve poor men sat while the sisters washed their feet, is still there, as are the dark entry and the wainscoted wall in the conference chamber. During John Eliot's day the famous walnut tree, mentioned as gigantic in 1599, flourished inside the open court. It was still alive and growing in 1710, and remembered in light rhyme almost a century later.

> Being such a size and mass
> And growing in so wise a college
> I wonder how it came to be
> It was not called the Tree of Knowledge.

Small in numbers in John Eliot's day, monastic in structure, lacking in strong leadership, Jesus College was for him the alma mater to whom many years later he sent the gift of his Indian Bible inscribed in Latin:

*Pro Collegio Jesu*

*Accipias mater quod alumnus humillimus filius,*
*oro preces semper habeus tuas offert.*

JOHANNES ELIOT

For Jesus College

Accept, Mother, I pray, what a most humble
alumnus offers, a son ever having thy prayers.

JOHN ELIOT

During his years of residence under her training, 1618–1622, the content of his studies was as medieval as the architecture of the buildings in which he lived and learned. Not only Jesus College but also all of the university was as yet untouched by the "new philosophy" which "calls all in doubt," as John Donne had written seven years earlier in his *An Anatomy of the World.*

Tis all in pieces, all coherence gone;
All just supply, and all Relation.
Prince, Subject, Father, Sonne, are things forgot.[12]

But not in Cambridge University. The medieval curriculum was as yet all but indestructible. The colleges not only presented a student with the materials for study, which were Aristotle and other relics of the ancient world, but also with the system (likewise Aristotelian) by which he would attack these materials. Scholasticism would shape his thinking for life.

Cambridge men in England or in New England carried the stamp in both matter and method in every sermon they preached. The goal of study is truth; yes, but truth is reached by dividing it from error. Cast your concept in the form of a question. Admit the opposite of what you set out to prove. Dispute it by a system of syllogistic reasoning. There are nineteen legitimate syllogistic forms and forty-five illegitimate ones. Make a *summa*. Harmonize opposites. Thus is truth tested and proved.

The lectures of the master, the guidance of the tutor and the disputations of students day after day exhibited these fundamentals in material and method. The result was familiarity with, and to some degree mastery of, some portions of ancient and medieval thought, agility in developing objections to the reasoning of one's rival, detecting fallacies, giving answers to answers, memorizing quotations which could be used in treatises and sermons—skills that lasted as long as the student lived. Not hospitality to new ideas, not experiment with the untried, but respect for authority was the result. The name of Ramus and his new methods of reasoning in attacking Aristotle were all but unknown until a generation after John Eliot's student days. Without books he would have learned by ear as his tutor read, and by long earnest exercise he would remember what he had heard longer than the next generation who would hold the book in their hands and read for themselves. Doubt would hardly nibble at the edges of what the master had taught. The dialectic of over four centuries had already established truth. To read John Eliot's story without remembering his training is to misjudge him. He belonged to his own day, both as a thinker and as interpreter of the Bible, which for preacher and layman was the fountain of all truth, and one interpreted it word for word as it was written, as though dictated by God Almighty.[13]

When he had been exactly two years at Jesus College, John Eliot's mother died. This was on March 16, 1620. Midway in his third year, November 21, 1621, his father also died. The loss of both parents left four children under fourteen in the home, one a newborn infant. Sister Sarah, the oldest daughter, was already the wife of William Curtis. Philip, the oldest son, was eighteen years old. By Bennett Eliot's will, executed only two weeks before his death, William Curtis, his son-in-law, was intrusted with responsibility for paying John Eliot's college expenses, and apparently there was no interruption to his studies. The excerpt concerning him from his father's will reads:

> I give and bequeath all the rents and profits of all my copy and customary lands and tenements in the several parishes of Ware, Hunsdon and Estweeke in the Co. of Harford. . . . for the space of eight years from the time of my decease quarterly to pay unto my son John Elliott the sum of eight pounds a year of lawful money of England for and toward his maintenance in the University of Cambridge where he is now scholar. . . .[14]

John Eliot took his degree, A.B., in 1622. University records make no mention of further residence toward a second degree before he is said (unofficially) to have applied for orders in 1625.

One remembers that this year, 1625, was the Great Plague Year, during which the work of the university was in almost complete paralysis. Infection had been brought to the quadrangles by a journeyman tailor, and when the plague "broke out in the Pantry" and the cook's son died, all regular work ceased. No lectures were given, stern precautions were taken and most of the students immediately departed. They did not return for nearly six months. The heads and a few others who remained barely had enough to eat during this grim interval, according to the report of tutor James Mede.

Whatever work John Eliot had been pursuing toward an M.A. degree prior to this outbreak would have been taken in course and would not have been recorded until the second degree was awarded. There is a strong likelihood that he did not return after the enforced interruption but instead that he was ordained and had some pulpit experience. His ordination record has not come to light despite diligent search by various scholars for many years. Very probably he would have received it from the Bishop of Ely, traditional patron of the nunnery of St. Radegund, before Jesus College was chartered on these foundations. Argument in favor of a regular ordination is based on his ready acceptance as "minister" when he arrived in Boston, Massachusetts, in 1631, and his immediate appointment to the pulpit of the First Church during the absence of its pastor, John Wilson. As early as 1631, ordination was the necessary qualification for such an appointment. Apparently, also, he came as no novice in the pulpit, although there would appear to be no extant scrap of record indicating what was his previous preaching experience in England.

In view of his lifework as preacher and man of religion, we should like to know what gave him the first impetus toward such a choice and, perhaps even more, what was his own personal religious experience as boy and young man. But of neither has any word come to light beyond his tribute to his parents and to Thomas Hooker, in whose school at Little Baddow he served briefly as usher immediately before Hooker's escape to Holland in July, 1630. This school, a temporary refuge for Hooker, was kept, according to Cotton Mather, in "his own hired house," where John Eliot was also living with the Hooker family during this time.

To this place was I called [John Eliot wrote] through the
infinite riches of God's mercy in Christ Jesus to my poor soul,
for here the Lord said to my dead soul, live! live! and through
the grace of God I do live and shall live forever! When I
came to this blessed family I then saw as never before, the
power of godliness in its lovely vigor and efficacy.[15]

In the light of John Eliot's lifelong record of service, the
words "in its lovely vigor and efficacy" define the spirit of his
own labors. He was not given to much speaking of his own
religious experience. Instead we see the "power of godliness"
expressed concretely in energetic, positive directions. Had he
kept a personal diary of his religious life during his college
days as was customary for young men, particularly those looking toward the ministry as a profession, his record would
hardly have shown such morbid self-examination by the day
and hour as John Ward's Cambridge diary, for example.[16]
This exhibit of a young man's doleful lamentation over such
lapses from the standard as a wandering mind during chapel,
Bible reading without proper thoughts, late rising on Sabbath, going to sleep without remembering that his last
thought should be of God, failing to pray before and after
meat and after the most inconsequential comings and goings,
make one wonder not only who set such a standard, but also
how a young man of intellectual capacity could take it so seriously. It is too frequent to have been the exceptional young
man's religiosity. Nothing in John Eliot's life hints at such
persistent self-interest, and one can only hope that he was not
exposed to it in some example at Jesus College. His tribute to
Thomas Hooker suggests something owed to their brief association at Little Baddow that strengthened his appreciation
for what was virile and positive in a man's religious faith.
Something virile and positive in his own nature had called
forth this appreciation. That his decision to embark for New
England may also have owed something to Thomas Hooker's

influence is a fair enough conjecture, but it is no more. Incentives to a young man in John Eliot's situation to emigrate in 1631 were manifold without the personal influence of anyone.

He was twenty-six years old when the Little Baddow school closed with Thomas Hooker's flight to Holland in 1630, and it was time for him to make a decision as to his own lifework. His formal training for the ministry was completed.[17] His eight-year allowance from his father's estate had been paid in full. He had met the young woman he hoped to marry. Another one-room school would have been easy to find, but apparently he felt that the schoolroom was not his place. He belonged in a pulpit. He was a Nonconformist, and good sense told him that with Archbishop Laud in power he would find no safe pulpit in England.

His decision was made in troubled times, for on all sides the surfaces of English life were sadly ruffled. The assassination of the king's favorite, the Duke of Buckingham, in 1628, had given voice to suppressed fears and growing antagonism to the Crown. The king's dissolving of Parliament in 1629 had aroused England afresh. There is no more shocking scene in Commons than on the day when at the king's command the sergeant at arms banged on the door until he broke it down, only to find the chamber empty and the session adjourned by the members' own quicker action. That banging on the door was heard all over England. During the eleven years before Parliament was again convened, Puritan leaders met secretly in every county of England and made their plans. One such meeting place in Essex was at Hatfield Broad Oak, seat of Sir Francis Barrington. Another was at Otes, seat of Sir William Masham. Young Oliver Cromwell, nephew of the widowed Lady Barrington, was a member of this group. Wise men, whether politicians or not, knew that war was coming, and soon.

To this Essex hotbed of Puritan sentiment came also members of the dissenting clergy who had plans to make. Meanwhile Laud's favor with the king increased, and with favor came increased power. Thomas Hooker had escaped in time, and John Cotton, less bold and widely influential, would escape also, though in disguise. Thomas Shepard would be silenced and unfrocked before he could take ship; Nathaniel Ward, Samuel Stone, Samuel Whiting would be suspended. So would many others who were to become New England's first generation. The ill fortune of those who were forcibly ejected from their pulpits was not noisily announced to the general public as yet, but both pulpit and pew were well aware of what was happening and they knew that the ax might fall anywhere. Younger ministers were looking ahead and making plans for the more distant future. As news came back from New England with each returning captain of John Winthrop's fleet, the New World became more real. For Puritans it also became the natural way out.

The immediate occasion for John Eliot's decision to sail is not recorded. We know only that when Captain Pierce weighed anchor in the late summer of 1631 and turned the ship *Lyon* out of the channel, John Eliot was one of those on board. He was the first of the Nazeing immigrants to embark for New England, and he did so with anticipation that family and friends would soon follow. He would land in the New World almost at the beginning of its settlement by Englishmen who had come not as explorers but as residents. Everything he had heard and read and dreamed about New England could hardly have prepared him for the first view of village Boston, nestled against Trimountain just beyond the marshes. Nor could imagination have dared even to suggest the challenge every day in this now eighteen-month-old colony would bring or the triumphs of first mastery.

## A PULPIT IN ROXBURY

AFTER a ten-week voyage Captain Pierce brought the ship
*Lyon* into Nantasket on November 2, 1631. "The wind
being contrary," John Winthrop wrote, "the ship stayed at
Long Island for the night," but next morning, "the wind
coming fair, she came to an anchor before Boston." The entire settlement and many of the people of the nearby towns
had come to greet the sixty passengers the ship brought. Unusual interest and hospitality, even a touch of gaiety attended
the welcome, for Margaret Winthrop, wife of the governor,
was on board with two of their children and three of Winthrop's by a former marriage. She had spent a year in preparation for coming. Many letters had been exchanged between
husband and wife, looking toward provision for a comfortable
voyage and the setting up of her household in Boston. Now
her safe arrival called forth a joyous welcome.

Governor Winthrop had gone on board for the night and
in the morning was brought to shore with his family by Captain Pierce in the ship's boat. As the little group stepped on
land, volleys of shot were fired and an armed guard advanced
as escort. Up Great Street (now State) they were led to the
wide marketplace where the crowd was waiting. Welcome was
further expressed to Madam Winthrop and her fellow passengers by the bringing of "great store of provisions, as fat hogs,
kids, venison, poultry, geese, partridges, etc., so as the like joy
and manifestations of love, had never been seen in New England." It was a great marvel, John Winthrop continued,
"that so much people and such store of provisions could be

gathered together at so few hours' warning." [1]   This abun-
dance of provision was the more noteworthy, for on his February arrival in this same year, Captain Pierce had brought
two hundred tons of provision in response to Governor Winthrop's urgent plea for supplies.  Some of the Boston residents
had died of scurvy and many more had been grievously ill.
The *Lyon* had arrived in time, however, for its cargo to save
many lives.  Meanwhile, another New England crop had been
harvested, and now on the fringe of this second winter the
health of the colony was generally very good.

In his *Journal* report of the passengers aboard the *Lyon* on
this November second arrival, John Winthrop spoke in the
third person, mentioning Margaret Winthrop as "the governor's wife," but calling his infant daughter, who had died on
the voyage, by her name, Anne.  He had never seen this child.
Of the other passengers he mentioned by name only "Mr.
John Eliot, a minister."  Quite likely the two men were not
strangers, but knew each other from some of the meetings before the governor's departure with his fleet in the preceding
spring.

John Eliot immediately took up residence in Boston.  On
the church book his name is on page 3; Margaret Winthrop's
name follows next.  It was now a year and a half since that
July day in 1630, when John Winthrop, Governor, Thomas
Dudley, Lieutenant Governor, Isaac Johnson and John Wilson had stood under a great oak in Charlestown and signed a
church covenant of their own making.  In part it read:

> "Wee whose names are here underwritten . . . do hereby
> solemnly, & religiously [as in His most holy Presence] Prom-
> ise, & bind orselves, to walke in all our wayes according to
> the Rule of the Gospell, & in all sincere Conformity to His
> holy Ordinances, & in mutual love & respect each to other,
> so long as God shall give us Grace." [2]

Since then, John Winthrop and others of the early arrivals had moved across the river to the Boston peninsula. John Wilson had been chosen pastor and had regularly preached to the congregation "in the umbrage of a great oak" when weather permitted, otherwise in the large fortlike structure built at the marketplace to accommodate the entire settlement at need. It would be almost another year before the first meetinghouse was built. For seven months now, since March, 1631, John Wilson had been back in England, trying to persuade his wife to come to Boston with him. The Boston people had been without a pastor although before Wilson left he had commissioned John Winthrop and several other lay leaders to continue the weekly "exercise of religion" during his absence, and they had done so. Weekly services had been held, the Scripture had been publicly read, the psalm sung and the congregation held together. Not without difficulty, however, for already the breath of heresy had come from the Watertown branch of the settlement.

The arrival of John Eliot, a minister, better schooled than laymen to confute error, seemed good fortune indeed, and the covenant members immediately invited him to be their substitute pastor until John Wilson returned. His acceptance was encouraging, for just before he arrived, Roger Williams had refused the same invitation. His answer had presaged controversy, perhaps deep trouble from his quarter, since he had contended that the Boston people being "unseparated," he could not serve them. What he meant, of course, was that so far the Boston congregation was still technically in communion with with the Anglican Church. Harmony, at least for the moment, was restored by John Eliot's acceptance of the post.

His preaching pleased the people, and when, on May 26, 1632, John Wilson returned (without his wife), the congre-

gation invited Eliot to remain as teacher, thereby completing
the pastoral office, as early New England conceived it. Had
he complied, Eliot's story and that of New England's mission
to the Indians might have been wholly different. His refusal
to accept Boston's offer, however, was not born of obstinacy or
lack of congeniality. His six months of initiation had passed
smoothly and his association with the Boston congregation
had been mutually pleasant. He refused because during these
six months the first company of the Nazeing people, his
friends and former neighbors had arrived and settled in Roxbury, two miles away, just across the narrow neck of land that
kept Boston from being an island. He had promised his
friends before he left England that if their plans to emigrate
were carried out and if he were still not permanently engaged
when they arrived, he would be their pastor. John Winthrop's account of what happened in this Boston-Roxbury situation was that "although Boston laboured all they could,
both with the congregation at Roxbury and with Mr. Eliot
himself," he could not be diverted from accepting the new
call.[3]

Various other New England first churches had been formed
similarly. Thirteen families had followed John Cotton, thirteen others Ezekiel Rogers; twelve had followed John Nor-
ton. "Mr. Hooker's company" from towns in the vicinity of
Braintree, Colchester, Chelmsford had come first, knowing
that as soon as he could leave safely, Thomas Hooker would
follow them as their pastor. The Boston congregation, of
course, understood John Eliot's refusal, but they regretted his
departure.

Roxbury received him joyfully. Roxbury church had been
gathered late in 1631 or early in 1632 (the first covenant is
lost), and the meetinghouse built immediately. Until it was
completed, Roxbury residents had worshiped with the Dor-

chester people. As in most early settlements, the meeting-house was "set on rising ground nigh unto some convenient trees" which afforded a supply of lumber. The name Meeting House Hill is still retained and this site has been used for the four later meetinghouses of the First Church Society. Here the beautiful fifth meetinghouse now stands.

The original structure was modest indeed. It measured only twenty by thirty feet, was built of squared logs neatly fitted together. The roof was thatched; the walls unplastered. It had no spire, no gallery, no pews and for a long time no floor. Worshipers sat on long benches without backs, the men on one side, the women on the other. Of course, there was no heat. Fifteen years later, a town vote ordered some repairs. In 1654 two galleries were added and the ends of the building were clapboarded. In 1658 "for greater warmth and comfort" the roof was shingled, and "for adornment" a pinnacle was built on either end. In 1673 a "nooning house" for the comfort of worshipers from a distance was ordered. Here on a winter Sunday they might enjoy a fire, warm food and a two-hour period of relaxation. This first meetinghouse served John Eliot's congregation for forty years. It was the heart of the town: a place of prayer, a refuge in time of danger, the center for transacting all civic business. It was "our meeting-house" to every man, woman, child in the town. As boy and young man John Eliot had known the beauty and sublimity of England's cathedrals. In his New England life this small, starkly plain structure stood for other values than architectural grandeur and costly ornament. He had put all that behind him.

He was formally dismissed from the Boston church November 5, 1632, one year and two days after his arrival in America. At first he was called teacher and later pastor, in Roxbury, a post he would continue to hold for the remainder of his life. Thomas Welde, the first pastor, was also an Essex man and a Cambridge graduate. He was nine years older than Eliot. Very probably the two men were already acquainted, as Thomas Welde had previously been minister in Terling, Essex, only a few miles from Nazeing.

The Roxbury membership at this date included an original nucleus from John Winthrop's company, consisting of five heads of families and one single man. Their names, as listed by Eliot, were William Pyncheon, often called founder of the town, Thomas Lambe, Thomas Rawlings, William Chase, George Alcock and William Porter. Together with wives and children, this group numbered twenty-five. Arrivals in 1631 and the spring of 1632 brought the total higher. The new settlers arriving from Nazeing made a considerable group with whom the newly appointed teacher had a common heritage. Others in succeeding years were also Essex men and women, some from Eliot's own family.[4]

His older sister, Sarah, wife of William Curtis, arrived with her husband and four of her children in 1632. Their oldest son, William, had come with John Eliot the year before. His sister Mary also came with William Curtis. Brother Philip who sailed later would also live in Roxbury. Brothers Francis and Jacob would join the Boston church. To live near these members of his own family and former neighbors, with other Essex friends as near as Watertown, Dorchester and Dedham would mean a life without the loneliness suffered by so many who had come alone. Pastor, teacher and a large share of the congregation were a transplanted people and to a degree considerably greater than in most early settlements.

For the newly selected teacher, the happiness of his transfer from Boston was increased by the arrival of his intended bride, Hanna Mumford, who came with his brother-in-law, William Curtis, in this same year. The wedding took place in

October, 1632, and in Roxbury records was the first marriage in the town. It would have been a festive occasion, as well as a community event of importance. At this date marriage was a civil rather than a religious ceremony in New England. On the first Sunday thereafter, the bride, attired in her wedding dress, would be escorted to her seat in the meetinghouse. As the bride of the teacher, Mistress Hanna would be taken to the front bench, at the right of the pulpit on the center aisle, known in all early meetinghouses as the minister's pew. It was as uncomfortable as all the other uncushioned benches, but in greater honor. Here Hanna Eliot would sit for the fifty-five years of Sundays this congregation would know her as the pastor's wife.

We should like to know more about Hanna Mumford Eliot. Tradition invests the Eliot home she graced, as one might expect, with the virtues celebrated in colonial homes, but no diary or journal spells these out for her individually in everyday reality. As wife and mother, tradition also makes her notably resourceful as head of a household that must be almost entirely self-sufficient; as hostess for unnumbered guests, many of whom would come uninvited and unheralded; as mother of the six children born into the home in the next fourteen years. Her service did not stop with her own household. Trained in physic and skillful in nursing, she also answered many an urgent call at her door, day and night. During her husband's regular weekly journeys to the Indians, she was in charge of the Eliot acres, which were extensive, and that her knowledge and skill in farm management might on occasion have overtopped his, various anecdotes testify. In her many-faceted partnership in the Eliot home she probably deserved the superlatives she inspired.

Fortunately, when the Roxbury story began for John Eliot in 1632, he had already had a full year's experience in New

England, enough to make him not quite a stranger to pioneer life. Except in the wintertime, the view out of his first house, built down the hill from the meetinghouse and on the margin of Stony Brook, was not greatly different from the English countryside he had known in his boyhood. Beyond the little cluster of houses were sloping fields, pastures, the river, deep woods in the farther distance. In this new settlement he now had a people to serve, a home, work to do, and he was ready for it.

So far as we know, he had accepted the post of teacher in this parish, with no idea beyond that of being a town minister for life. Nor is there anything at this date to suggest the special intellectual gifts, originality, imagination and practical genius later activities reveal. He found the work for which America remembers him by living in this small newly settled town as one of its pioneers. When a wider door opened, he walked through it and found still wider doors. His later conviction that he had an obligation to preach to the Indians of the Algonquian tribe became all-consuming and his dedication unique. Conviction and dedication called forth powers he did not know he possessed and made his contribution eminent. But for the next ten or twelve years after his arrival his thought and energies belonged primarily to the small Roxbury company he had come to serve.

Times of harmony in the relationship between pastor and people often leave few records, and so it was in these first years of the Roxbury church. The earliest record is little more than a list of members, baptisms, marriages, deaths, censures and forgiveness after repentance, such as one finds in nearly every town of early New England for the first generation. Roxbury's records are somewhat more straggling and imperfect than many others, because here as in far too many early towns, fire destroyed the house in which records were kept. We have the item about this Roxbury fire in John

Eliot's hand. It started in the house of John Johnson. "Toward the end of the first month call'd march; there happened (by God's p'vidence,) a very dreadfull fire in Roxbury streets, none knoweth how it was kindled, but being a very fierce wind, it suddenly p'vailed." [5] Seventeen or eighteen barrels of powder, the settlement's entire supply, being stored in Johnson's house, blew up, scattering the flames and preventing anyone from getting near enough to save anything of the contents. Barns and outhouses, many and great, were completely destroyed before the wind turned. "Sundry houses [were] set on fire by the blow, & yet all quenched, through God's rich mercy in Christ." [6] So says the record.

The old town book and possibly also the earliest church book were lost. The extant early records, John Eliot's substitute for the lost book, were probably written down the year after the fire in an effort to preserve what could be remembered from the earlier story. Tradition has it that the residents assembled at the pastor's request and that each one supplied an account of his own family as to births, marriages, deaths and such other personal data as were thought worthy of preservation. The resulting record is, of course, very different from what it would have been if written down at its proper date. The order is not always chronological. Many blanks are left where dates or names should be, probably because family memories could not recall them.

This scrappy record, however, tells a story of beginnings which is more than names and dates. A seventeenth-century minister was asking the questions, and from both his questions and the answers he received, one who can read understandingly finds a religious belief, a social order, a pattern of life. It was a pattern which little knots of men and women living in clusters of new houses over vast unsettled spaces struggled passionately to maintain. Not only whole chapters of American historical background are written into such tangled records, but if they are read discerningly, here is the beginning of what we call the American character, stripped bare to the bone. Underneath these brief items lies a framework of belief unquestioned; of conviction, of courage and the iron of resolve, all but impregnable.

Let samples of the record speak.[7]

> Valentine Prentiss, he came to this land in the yeare, 1631, & joyned to the church in the yeare 1632. he brought but one child to the Land, his son John, & buryed anoth[r] at sea; he lived a godly life, and went through much affliction by bodyly infirmity. & died leaving a good sav[r] of godlyness behind him.

> John Ruggles he came to N.E. in the yeare 1635, & soone after his coming joyned to the church, he was a lively christian, knowne to many of the church, in old England where many of the church injoyed society together: he brought his first borne John Ruggles w[h] him to N.E. & his second son was still-borne, in the 11th month 1636, of w[h] his wife dyed.

> Barbara Ruggles, the wife of John Ruggles. She was a Godly Christian woman, & joyned to the church w[h] her husband, the pow[r] of the grace of Christ did much shine in her life & death, she was much afflicted w[h] the stone chollik in w[h] sicknesse she manifested much patience, and faith; she dyed in childbed, the 11th month, 1636, & left a godly savor behind her. These two broke the knot first of the Nazing christians, I meane they first died of those christians yt came from yt towne in England.

> John Mathews. He was convicted of notorious drunkennes & cast out of ye church l.of 3[m] 1659. But afterw[d] restored agn upon his repentance.

—— Stebbins the wife of Martin Stebbins. She was so vyolent in her passion. yt she offered vyolence to her husband, wʰ being divulged, was of such infamy, yᵗ she was cast out of o Church but soone after she humbled her selfe & was received in againe.

1646    Obadiah Gore a child of 10 years dyed of a Consumption
Mo 1    wᵗʰ as sweete & gracious expʳessions of faith as ev we
day 7   have heard.

day 23  Bro. Griggs who lay in a long affliction of sicknesse & shined like gold in it, greatly glorifying God & magnifying his grace in Christ.

1675    Dorothy Swan, she expʳessed signes of faith above o measure of such an infant being but 2 years and half old.

Thomas Hills a man servant. he came in the years 1633. he lived among us in good esteeme & Godly, & dyed about the 11 to 12ᵗʰ month, 1634 and left a good savor behind him, he was a very faithfull & prudent servant, & a good christian, he dyed in mʳ Eliots family.

John Stow he arrived at N.E. the 17ᵗʰ of the 3ʳᵈ month ano 1634. he brought his wife & 6 children: Thomas, Elizabeth, John, Nathaniel, Samuel, Thankfull.

Elizabeth Stow, the wife of John Stow, she was a very goodly matron, a blessing not only to her family and to all the church and when she had lead a christian conversation a few years among us she dyed and left a good savor behind her.

Occasionally, John Eliot adds livelier details about some of the notorious sinners. There was, for example, the entry of the two ungodly servants of John Moody, "especially one of them; who in his passion would wish himselfe in hell; he used desperate words, yet had a good measure of knowledge." One

night, against their master's counsel, they went to the oyster
bank in a boat, stayed all night, and in the morning at low
tide when they were gathering oysters, their boat was carried
beyond their reach.  In their fright they shouted to the land,
"but being very early and remote [their cries] were not heard
till the water had risen very high upon them to the arm-
holes."  Too late a man on Meeting House Hill heard them;
he cried, ran to the shore, swam to their boat and hastened to
them, "but alas they were both so drowned, before any help
could possibly come, a dreadful example of God's displeasure
against obstinate servants."

There was also Goodwife Webb:

> the wife of William Webb.  She followed baking &
> through her covetuous mind she made light waight after
> many admonitions, and after sundry rebuks of o Court,
> & officers in the market . . . . . . as also for an habit of
> lying & shifting, after much admonition, & also for a
> grosse ly in publik, flatly denying y$^t$ after she had
> weighed her dough, she never nimed off bitts from each
> loaf, w$^h$ was by 4 witnesses testified . . . for all w$^h$
> grosse sins she was excommunicated the 23 day of the 8
> month, ano 1642, her ways having bene long a greif of
> heart to her Godly neighbors.  But afterward she was
> reconciled to ye Church & lived christianly & dyed com-
> fortably.

So did many other of the erring ones in the small world of
pioneer Roxbury.  Between the lines one may read the guiding counsels of the pastor.

Long chapters in life stories are half-hidden, half-revealed
in some of the most frequently repeated phrases in these brief
records: to take hold of the covenant, to be a lively Christian,
humble in rebuke, to die and leave a good savor behind.

Thus did one fulfill the law of God, and at the end enter into life everlasting. Even those who fell into gross sin, were stubborn in rebuke and had to be delivered over to Satan could be restored again after their penitence, enjoy the fellowship of the "visible saints" and also gain heaven in the end.

John Eliot includes himself and his wife in this membership roll, ending the brief outline of his life to 1646 with the names and baptisms of his six children, Hannah, John, Joseph, Samuel, Aaron and Benjamin, who was born 29th of the 11th month, 1646. This date, one year after the fire, approximately fixes the time at which the reconstructed history was written down. In this same year, Thomas Welde, pastor since 1632, was sent as colony agent to England and did not return. Thereafter, John Eliot was in full charge of the parish for four years and probably for this reason had felt responsibility for restoring the earlier record.

Something of the spirit of his entire ministry is in these brief entries. His people were his care and he knew them. His standards of Christian character were inflexible, but his approach to the erring ones was unfailingly kind.

His own faith in God's providential protection was literal. When the wife of Peniel Brown, who lived on a farm some distance from town, was delivered of a child "by God's mercy w$^t$out the help of any oth$^r$ woman," it was "God himself helping his pore servants in a straight." When in 1646 the caterpillars came in "suddaine, innumerable armys," devouring whole meadows of grass, barley, wheat, fields of corn, crossing the highways by thousands, "much prayer was made to God about it, with fasting in diverse places & the Lord heard, & on a suddaine took ym all away againe in all pts of the country, to the wonderment of all men: it was of the Lord, for it was done suddainly." [8]

Marvels always had special emphasis: strange symptoms of

disease, deliverances, whatever was uncommon, particularly what seemed unnatural—hailstones as large as musket balls, a sudden turn of the wind just in time to save a house from fire, an epidemical sickness. In all of these, "God's rods are teaching," it was "as if the Lord had immediately sent forth an angel." [9]

The emphasis on positive qualities persists throughout this pastoral record. The ideal comes through even in some of the briefest reports of these men and women of good esteem among us, prudent servants and faithful, godly throughout life and of good conversation among us. After Samuel Danforth's handwriting begins, when he came as colleague pastor, the entries are briefer; we miss the adjectives and phrases of commendation which have given life to the earlier story.

During these early years John Eliot began his long leadership in local affairs in the town, none more notable than his share in the founding of the Roxbury grammar school. The date is uncertain since the original *Agreement* signed by the sponsors was destroyed in the fire of 1645. A copy of this *Agreement,* dated "last day of august, 1645," is extant on the first page of the *Old School Book,* possessed by the present school.

Sometimes spoken of as the oldest grammar school in America, Roxbury Latin School (as is carefully noted by its latest historian) [10] is the oldest American free and independent school "in continuous existence," although even this more precise phrase is still challenged by the Boston Latin School, founded ten years earlier and probably not closed for a full year during the Revolution. Quibbling aside, however, Roxbury Latin School came early to a town of perhaps sixty families from whom, according to Governor Winthrop's record, "every inhabitant bound some house or land for a yearly allowance for ever." [11] This system of private support through land endowment had been brought over from England and was common in the colony during the decade of the 1640's. Support by taxation for public schools came later.

John Eliot's name is second in the 1645 *Agreement,* and his is the fourth subscription. Governor Thomas Dudley had signed first and there are forty-two signatures after John Eliot's. The Massachusetts Education Law, passed in 1642, put responsibility on every parent to see to it that every child in the family and every apprentice under his roof be taught to read and write. By 1642 there were already four children in the Eliot home, and nearly every other home in the town could muster a group of candidates for schooling. It was time to begin making plans.

John Eliot has often been called founder of the Roxbury Latin School, but he would have insisted that this was a shared effort. His inspiration and his energetic labors are on every page of its early history. His faith in education was absolute, and his never-ending efforts to found still one more school offer one of the most illuminating clues to the understanding of his spirit. Whenever he preached to a new company of Indians, the next time he came he organized a school for them and their children. He trained native teachers and always more than were immediately needed, so that he might have a teacher ready for the next town to be founded. When he was aged and too feeble even to walk up Meeting House Hill on Sabbath, he collected the Indian and Negro children of his neighborhood and taught them to read and write. Cotton Mather remembered his prayer at a synod meeting in Cambridge and recorded it in his tribute to Eliot in these words:

Lord for schools every where among us! That our schools may flourish! That every member of this assembly may go

home and procure a good school to be encouraged in the
town where he lives! That before we die, we may be so happy
as to see a good school encouraged in every plantation of
the country! [12]

His older brother Philip Eliot was the first master of the
Roxbury grammar school. It was a one-room school then,
with a few boys aged six to twelve in the first throes of learning to read and speak Latin or "Good Literature" as it was
called in the *Agreement*. Any boy in the town might learn
there, and those who survived its intellectual rigors were po-
tential entrants at Harvard. John Eliot's major services
through the years came at times of crisis. After the founding,
they came in the long struggle with the town to maintain the
school's independence of outside control; they came legally,
with the 1670 action confirming the original *Agreement*.
They came also financially, notably by a donation from the
legacy to John Eliot of all the property in New England
owned by Thomas Bell, once a member of the Roxbury
church. With the larger portion of this legacy, Eliot founded
a second Roxbury Latin School in Jamaica Plain. This school
also was "free and independent," marking one more important chapter in John Eliot's services to American education.
Preaching being a major concern of the pastor, it is unfortunate that none of his sermons appears to have survived either in print or manuscript. Even the one election sermon he
was invited to preach (1659) was not ordered printed. We
depend therefore on mere scraps preserved here and there in
letters and on occasional reports of his contemporaries as to
his pulpit matter and style. Among these Cotton Mather,
young enough to be Eliot's son, wrote most fully. Making
allowance for the Mather extravagance, it would appear from
his description that John Eliot's sermon was very simple. Cal-

vinistic doctrine asks something of the adult mind, but apparently Eliot could interpret it simply enough so that the "lambs of the flock" could follow him. In his reported answers to the questions asked by his Indian hearers, he often used concrete analogies which he never seemed to lack, and doubtless his pulpit sermons in Roxbury showed this gift also.

Some enlightenment also comes from his advice to other preachers. Were their sermons "well-studied"? Did they show "good thinking and good reading"? From his mention of his own reading, one gathers that a large part of it concerned biblical exegesis, as was natural enough in his day. His great textbook was the Bible, always the Bible, and although this was generally true of his contemporary preachers as well, John Eliot excelled among them in biblical knowledge and ability to use it instantly.

From Cotton Mather's description[13] we picture him as speaking extemporaneously, perhaps without even notes with him in the pulpit. His delivery was graceful and warm, with crescendoes of vigor if sin were being rebuked, or "God's trumpets of wrath against all vice" being sounded. Then he became a veritable Boanerges, speaking with "a most penetrating liveliness" and making words into thunderbolts. The most revealing quality in his sermons, as one gathers it from Mather's many encomiums, is that they had in them something "beside and beyond the meer study of man." However one may interpret these words, they suggest something of power in his preaching, something not easy to analyze, compulsive, deeply inner, something of the man's personality, to which people of all ages and backgrounds responded. Whatever it was, it was John Eliot's secret which he probably did not know he possessed.

Occasionally he spoke militantly from his pulpit on something he considered wrong in the conduct of public affairs.

One such occasion came in 1634, his third year at Roxbury, and concerned the treaty of amity made with the Pequots who were facing war with the Narragansets. Governor Winthrop, after consultation in Boston with ministers, had arranged this treaty without asking the consent of the people. John Eliot, who loved democracy, spoke against this act with such spirit that (according to Winthrop's entry in his *Journal*) "he caused the people to take occasion to murmur against us for it." Representation in government was at this time an issue of concern to Massachusetts colonists, which explains both the people's murmuring and the governor's alarm because of it. A committee of ministers was immediately appointed to deal with the Roxbury teacher and show him his error.[14]

John Eliot was tractable, admitted that his criticism had been mistakenly applied in that this treaty agreed to friendship and peace instead of war, for which consent of the people would have been imperative. From his pulpit on the following Sunday he acknowledged his error, carefully stating the area within which the people should be consulted. He had really changed his view as to their fundamental right not a whit; he merely reported his enlightenment as to this particular case. His admission of error was not the act of a timid man, but of a strong one. He had cleared himself of blame and also increased his stature with his people.

First generation ministers held office for life in New England, and through John Eliot's fifty-eight years in Roxbury, there is no record that his people would have wished it to be otherwise. The pastor and people lived not only in harmony but in mutual affection. When John Eliot was too infirm to preach to them, he said, "I do here give back my salary." Of course, they refused it, appointed a successor and paid both men. But that was a far-distant time as the decade of the 1640's came in.

## A VOICE AT
## ANNE HUTCHINSON'S TRIAL

ROXBURY CONCERNS were not the whole of the young minister's thought and labors. In addition to preaching and the pastoral care of his people, John Eliot also had a share with other colony ministers in the civil and religious affairs of the Boston region. His counsel was often asked by governor and magistrates, and his presence expected in assemblies concerning civil matters. Reciprocally, turmoils in matters religious were the responsibility of governor and magistrates. Town and parish were one as were commonwealth and meetinghouse, and no community was separate unto itself alone. The governor of the colony was defender of the faith as well as protector and head of the commonwealth. The clergy stood at his right hand and shared responsibility for both.

Turmoils local and general had come from the very beginning. Undesirables had either been severely punished or gotten rid of. Thomas Morton, a pestilent fellow, had been sent back to England twice before John Eliot arrived and his maypole had been demolished. He would return. Philip Ratcliffe had been publicly whipped for "wickedness" (unnamed) and for using words some thought "deserved death." He had had his ears cut off. "I saw it done," wrote gentle, righteous Roger Clap. Such incidents as had a savor of the sensational were sometimes remembered, but the scores of common garden-variety iniquities were forgotten as soon as the punishment had been suffered.

But to both clergy and magistrate, heresy in the covenanted

circle was worse than the most heinous offenses that called for the whipping post or put the offender's feet in the bilboes. Nor could heresy be ended by punishment. Before ten years had passed and in nearly every meetinghouse heretics had been delivered up to Satan and cast out for some whisper of unorthodox belief. Usually offenders repented, confessed their errors publicly and were either forgiven or joined some other church circle to begin anew. What neither clergyman or magistrate seemed to realize was that the challenge of each pioneer day not only encouraged independence of thought and action but also demanded it. To find a better way to do nearly everything than was used yesterday was a compelling urge, or pioneers could hardly even have survived. Why not think independently in religious matters also? No, said religious leaders and magistrates alike. Doctrine must remain the same. Revelation is finished. New ideas in religion are contraband and let no one dare advance them. John Robinson had known better, but his freer advice to the Plymouth Pilgrims was not being heard in Boston. The clergy were adamant. Given time, numbers alone would defeat them, as heterodoxy came in every new shipload of colonists.

Most heresy cases were first handled locally. The individual church dealt with offenders and if evidence was conclusive and penitence genuine, the case was closed. But in 1637, and long before court action was taken against them, John Wheelwright and Anne Hutchinson had become the worried concern of nearly every minister and magistrate in the colony, particularly in the Boston region. The poison of unorthodoxy had become more than a taint; it was a danger openly faced. Every watchman in every parish became more alert and more suspicious. Sermons were preached against the new ideas, but most of them missed the mark and merely whetted the appetite of listeners who desired to know more about these new and dangerous ideas.

Roxbury had already had specific cases of heresy, but fortunately for pastor and teacher the accused had moved away before their cases became serious enough to call for a review by the General Court. Mary Dummer, wife of Richard Dummer, moved to Newbury and declared her views there. Philip Sherman went to "the Iland" where he continued to "behave sinfully in these matters," and was "cast out" by the island church. Thomas Wilson in 1638, during the Anne Hutchinson troubles, went into exile with Thomas Wheelwright, and Roxbury again escaped publicity in disciplining an erring member.

Boston was not so fortunate. Its "cases" did not move elsewhere. Almost from the day of her coming, Anne Hutchinson had made trouble. John Cotton, colleague pastor with John Wilson in the Boston church, had been the magnet that drew her to New England. She had previously attended his church in Lincolnshire, England, and a year after Cotton came to New England she had followed him with her husband and large family in order to continue under his ministry. This fact alone need not have been surprising, as Cotton was perhaps the most gifted pulpit man in New England at this date, and his sermons were widely praised.

Anne Hutchinson's earlier history offers some explanations of the turmoil of which she was soon the center in Boston.[1] She was born Anne Marbury, daughter of Francis Marbury of Lincolnshire, a dissenting minister whose rashness of judgment and harsh criticism of the settled clergy had put him in Marshalsea prison for a time, and before he was finally silenced, had forced him to move from one parish to another. In consequence, his daughter had lived a stormy life throughout her childhood. Under her father's dominating influence and guidance she had acquired a familiarity with the Bible unusual for her years, and also in her youth she had developed a skill in disputation and an ambition to use it publicly. This ambition had possibly been fired by her knowledge of a woman evangelist on the "Isle of Ely" long before her time. It was recalled by Hugh Peter in his testimony at Anne Hutchinson's trial that she had mentioned this unnamed woman preacher in one of his conferences with her. William Hutchinson, husband of Anne, was a successful tradesman, to whom she had already borne fifteen children before she came to New England at the age of forty-three.

Immediately upon arrival she and her husband and her brother-in-law, John Wheelwright, were admitted to the Boston church, thereby securing a place in the community. In addition, Anne Hutchinson's skill with medicines and in nursing, together with her willingness to go wherever she was needed, made her welcome at once in many Boston homes. Of course, she talked of religion, and the novelty of a woman, not a black robed minister, as a religious teacher was electric with the women of the settlement. In a few months she was the talk of the town. In the beginning most of this talk was favorable. What she had to say seemed to be guaranteed by the authority of the Scriptures in which her knowledge was impressive. Her facility with Bible texts astonished her hearers. Her insistence that the test of religion was inner, not outer, also seemed well within the white lines of safety. The *covenant of grace* as opposed to the *covenant of works* was her favorite theme. This was a distinction well known to, and to some extent understood by, the laity almost anywhere in New England at that date, especially in the congregation of John Cotton.

Finespun and endlessly complicated as the theories of grace appear to those unversed in theology, to seventeenth-century church members one may suppose that the phrase *covenant of grace* spelled something fairly simple. *Grace* was a divine gift. A *covenant* was a contract, and to be included in this relationship with God Almighty meant for the individual professing Christian at least a measure of assurance of eternal salvation. It was God-given, inner, invisible. By contrast, the *covenant of works* gave man a chance for divine favor by his own good behavior in this world. It was outer, visible, seen of men. Orthodoxy demanded the *covenant of grace*. It was one step in the redemption experience, and in her ardent championship of it as fundamental, Anne Hutchinson was one of the elect. Ironically, however, she put herself among the outcasts, not by theological error, but by her own bad judgment as she became personal in criticism of the settled clergy.

Inevitably suspicion against her began to arise in Boston, as soon as she dared to call names. At first she had met inquirers in her parlor once a week, then twice, often using the sermon of John Wilson the Sunday before as her subject. Her interpretation of the text was not always the same as his, and her eloquence in defending her view won a response from her hearers. More and more the discussions sloped toward the opposed doctrines of *grace* and *works*. Pastor Wilson became alarmed. She was almost a rival. Soon differences of interpretation became clearly criticism of Wilson. He was preaching a *covenant of works*. She was making the *covenant of grace* the better way. More of his congregation came to her parlor week after week until the procession winding there from all corners aroused a stronger suspicion. Most of all, the fact that aristocratic Henry Vane, young, charming, and almost from the day of his arrival popular with all classes — leading men, merchants, apprentices and all ranks in between — was sympathetic to her views spelled danger in more insistent terms. In the election of 1636, when Vane unseated John Winthrop as governor and became leader of the colony, official Boston and the clergy of the entire region were deeply apprehensive. Would Anne Hutchinson's influence gain by an alliance that

had now become politically powerful? The very foundations
of the commonwealth seemed unstable. What next?

Anne Hutchinson's immediate move proved to be even
bolder than any she had yet made. She pronounced indictment of the entire New England clergy except her brother-in-
law and John Cotton. All except these two were preaching
the *covenant of works.* No minister except these two was
"sealed of the Spirit," and therefore not an "able minister of
the Gospel." In those days criticism of the clergy amounted
to sedition and was an affair for the civil authorities as well as
the church. Furthermore, she increased the seriousness of her
offense by claiming as the source of her accusation, God's own
revelation to her soul. Not the judgment of her mind, but an
inner voice, God's voice to her personally. Antinomianism in
the very heart of New England. This was another theological
term which in popular thought was little more than a frightened memory of the Peasants' Rebellion of Münster, a century before. Slumbering unrest in the church body and
throughout Boston soon led to vague fears and open discord.
Mistress Hutchinson's adherents were a party within the membership, sharply divided from the orthodox group that upheld John Wilson. Both sides became vocal. The phrases
*covenant of works* and *covenant of grace* became passwords of
identification. One could hear them at the docks, on the
street, in the marketplace as well as in Anne Hutchinson's
parlor. Both sides searched their Bibles in agreement with
her criticism of the ministry or against them.

John Winthrop was, of course, with the orthodox party.
Not a man of imagination, no voyager into the realm of the
intangible, he was stability itself as to the religious purposes
and goals of the Massachusetts Bay Colony. No hardship was
too severe, no price too high for their maintenance. In his
concept the "city set on a hill" demanded like-mindedness in

every householder up and down every street in the settlement. Dissent from the common aim would be fatal to the
stability of the state. Briefly in the beginning there had been
unity in that small company that had listened to Winthrop's
lay sermon on the deck of the flagship *Arbella,* as it neared
the New England coastline, or had heard of it later from the
passengers. Varied in background, diverse in their individual
purposes in coming, these first immigrants had to some extent
shared the confidence that God had made them a place in this
new world, and that life here would be different and better
than all they had known in the homeland. The unifying element had been religious and it had been strengthened week
by week as they had listened to the Sunday sermon. Anne
Hutchinson's branding of the colony ministers as "unsealed"
had struck at the very center of this fundamental unity.

As the breach widened, each party grew bolder. At a
church meeting, October 30, 1636, a member of the Hutchinson group proposed that John Wheelwright be made associ-
ate pastor with John Cotton over the Boston flock. John
Winthrop was instantly on his feet in protest. His words rang
out. "The church being well furnished already with able
ministers whose spirits we know; and whose labours God has
blessed in much love and sweet peace, it is not fitting to call
one whose spirit we do not know and who seems to dissent in
judgment." [2] John Wheelwright was not chosen, but peace
was not restored by his rejection nor was the sting of the
Hutchinson criticism lessened.

By next election time the orthodox party was no longer on
the defensive; they had organized a positive and practical
plan of action, and they had done it so well that it worked.
The place of balloting was changed at the last minute from
Boston to Cambridge. John Wilson was boosted up on the
lower branches of a great tree, from which he electioneered

lustily for John Winthrop as the Boston voters hurried by, with the result that Henry Vane was defeated and Winthrop again elevated to the governor's chair. The Hutchinsonians were surprised and angry. Shortly afterward, Henry Vane, realizing that his short day of power was over, took ship and returned to England to grow to full manhood, give twenty-five years of service to his country and at the end by his martyr-dom on Tower Hill to write one of the noblest pages of the English Restoration years. His departure from New England on August 3, 1637, cleared the way for the orthodox party to deal with Anne Hutchinson, who in Winthrop's words, was "the breeder and nourisher of all these distempers."

Her brother-in-law, John Wheelwright, provided the open-ing. His remarks on a day of prayer and fasting, January 19, 1637, when he was asked to speak a few words following John Wilson's sermon, were a call to battle.[3] His fate and Anne Hutchinson's were sealed from that hour.

One reads the ensuing story of this bold woman before her judges remembering that in 1637 Massachusetts was barely seven years old and that a system of justice for offenders be-fore the law had not as yet been fully worked out. Not until fifty years later would she have needed to be formally indicted and to have had legal counsel and a jury trial. In 1637 she had none of these safeguards. One remembers that in a so-ciety in which church and state were one, both civil and ec-clesiastical bodies had authority to bring her to trial. With the General Court, it was the safety of the state that was of direct concern. Anne Hutchinson was guilty of sedition. With the Boston church, the issue was the security of estab-lished doctrine. Patient human sympathy toward an erring member of the community mattered to neither body. Hence the harshness that another day finds almost incredible.

John Eliot, along with his brother ministers and magis-

trates in 1637, had a determining voice in the destruction of
the unfortunate woman, and long as his life was yet to be, he
did not live long enough to think differently of the verdict in
which he had shared. Harshness was not his role with offenders, and nothing harsh is recorded of his part in either of these
two trials, civil or ecclesiastical. Angry voices were raised in
both of them, but not John Eliot's. Gentleness of manner,
kindness of feeling were habitual with him and he showed
them combined with an inflexibility of judgment wherever
unsoundness of doctrine was concerned. Truth, as he saw it,
was to be found within the covers of the Bible and he knew by
chapter and verse where to find it. In Anne Hutchinson's
trials, it was the knife-blade logic by which he had been
trained to separate truth from error, his memory for Scripture
texts, and also the practical sense by which he knew when to
use the evidence he possessed, that made Eliot's role significant.

His Roxbury colleague, Thomas Welde, was a man of very
different temper, an acute reasoner, also an ardent student
of the Bible, skillfully using texts in their strictly literal application, but his attitude toward offenders in doctrine was
that of a harsh accuser and judge. His vindictive attitude toward Anne Hutchinson is plain to see in his account of her
trial for heresy in his book, *A Short Story of the rise, reign,
and ruine of the Antinomians.* He was merciless in condemnation. His inordinate zeal for strict orthodoxy reflects precisely the mood of the John Wilson faction in the Boston
church when the trials were the events of the hour.

Action against Anne Hutchinson was in three parts. First
came the calling of a synod. It assembled in Cambridge on
August 30, and lasted for three weeks.[4] The members of the
New England clergy and leading laymen from each church
took part, and the purpose was to divide truth from current

error. The first week was given to the listing of errors reported from all sources by ministers or laymen. A harvest of
eighty-two errors was garnered. To a later day many of these
seem dusty indeed, but not to this gathering in 1637. The
various stages of religious conversion, particularly the posi-
tion of faith in the process was an issue, not a theological
tenet. Was faith a means toward securing salvation or a result? Does the assurance of the Holy Spirit do away with the
evidence of "good works" to prove that a man is saved? What
is the difference between *soul* and *spirit?* Does the soul die
with the body?

Each one of all the eighty-two errors was carefully as-
sessed, debated and entered on the list. Emphasis was on the
idea, not upon the person accused, but sometimes personali-
ties were plain to see. Names were called, rebukes administered from the chair and apologies demanded.

John Cotton was probably the most uncomfortable member of the gathering, for Anne Hutchinson's praise of him so
lavishly given had made him suspect by his brother ministers,
who might easily have been (perhaps unconsciously, let us
say) jealous of him as well. He was a more impressive
preacher than any of them and well deserved the popularity
his sermons had won for him in the Boston region as well as
in the homeland. He was also more subtle in argument than
most of his fellows, and the literalness of the synodical attack
on alleged error gave him a chance to use subtlety in escape.
He had a genius for compromise and a habit of hedging
when danger came too close. He would need both in this
tussle. Neither the compromise nor the hedging spelled unorthodoxy; not at all. They merely revealed a mind that did
not see black and white so unmistakably as John Wilson saw
them.

When the eighty-two charges were at last assembled, and

every one of them clearly adjudged an error, "What shall we do with them?" called out the moderator.

"Let them go to the devil of hell whence they came," shouted John Wilson, chief sufferer of them all. His grievance against Anne Hutchinson was deeply personal as well as doctrinal. She had almost removed his crown, and his words and actions during the three weeks had betrayed his emotions many times. Before adjournment was voted, the synod went on record as agreeing that her weekly meetings were "disorderly and without rule." Thomas Hooker, who had been moderator for a time and had sensed the hard feeling against her, sent back word from Hartford, advising moderation in treating those under suspicion. Her other judges, however, would forget this admonition.

Four days after the adjournment of the synod, new elections were ordered in the colony, and to the surprise of the voting freemen, fifteen new members were elected to the General Court and seventeen reelected. This change of personnel left everyone wondering what the action of the newly elected Court would mean in the Hutchinson-Wheelwright crisis. The orthodox party, however, was reassured. The first business before the Court concerned John Wheelwright. He was called to acknowledge his offensive remarks in his Fast Day sermon. Refusing even to appear, he was disfranchised, disarmed and banished from the colony, with only fourteen days to settle his affairs before departure. Intimidated by this stern verdict, thirty of the seventy-five men who had signed a petition affirming confidence in his innocence came at once to Governor John Winthrop, confessing error in supporting him. Their confession was honored and they retained the privilege of freemen. The remaining forty-five men were disarmed and disfranchised. Several among them who were defiant were also banished with John Wheelwright. This Court action boded ill for Anne Hutchinson whose turn came next. Even in advance of the session which would hear her case, some of her adherents changed sides. Clearly her case was lost before she was called. She was one woman alone before the authority and power of both state and church. She had no legal counsel, no jury, and she was not even formally accused of a stated crime.

Her trial was called.[5] The meetinghouse was crowded, the air tense, Governor Winthrop in the chair. He read the charge against her. "Mistress Hutchinson, you are called here as one of those that have disturbed the peace of the commonwealth and the churches here: . . . you have spoken divers things . . . very prejudicial to the honour of the churches and ministers thereof, and you have maintained a meeting and an assembly in your house that hath been condemned by the general assembly as a thing not tolerable nor comely in the sight of God nor fitting for your sex, and notwithstanding that was cried down, you have continued the same, therefore we have thought good to send for you to understand how things are, that if you be in an erroneous way we may reduce you. . . . otherwise if you be obstinate in your course that then the court may take such course that you trouble us no further, therefore I would intreat you to express whether you do not justify Mr. Wheelwright's sermon and the petition." Her answer established that she considered herself no meek culprit before them. "I am called here to answer before you but I hear no things laid to my charge."

> Governor: "I have told you some already and more I can tell you."
>
> Mrs. Hutchinson: "Name one, sir."
>
> Governor: "Have I not named some already?"
>
> Mrs. Hutchinson: "What have I said or done?"

This beginning established the pattern of her responses for the two day session that followed. Instead of answering Governor Winthrop's direct questions directly, she replied by asking him questions, made adroit evasions, gave flat denials or offered a comment that turned the direction of the exchange. Once she sent back what amounted almost to a counter accusation: "I did not come hither to answer to questions of that sort." More than once when pushed into a corner she flashed back: "Prove that." Obviously in verbal sparring, she was more than a match for John Winthrop and for John Endicott and Simon Bradstreet, both of whom tried to help the governor. Deputy Governor Dudley was more successful but only because he was willing to be more ruthless in outwitting the accused woman. Time after time she slipped out of a trap designed to bring an admission that would condemn her. In one apparently futile moment Winthrop said: "It is well discerned to the Court that Mrs. Hutchinson can tell when to speak and when to hold her tongue." But not quite, as soon appeared.

The six ministers who had conferred with her during the preceding months were called to testify to her criticism of all the clergy except John Cotton and John Wheelwright. John Eliot was one of those included in her condemnation. She delayed this testimony which she knew would be against her by demanding that the witnesses testify under oath.

"An oath is an ordinance of God," John Winthrop reminded her.

"That is the thing I desire," she answered. Some parley ensued. Ministers should be believed without an oath. John Eliot ended the parley by saying: "If the Court calls us out to swear, we will swear." Hugh Peter, Thomas Welde and John Eliot were sworn.

Further delay came when the witnesses Anne Hutchinson had brought in her favor were called first, John Cotton being one of these. His testimony, given in what was probably one of the most uncomfortable moments of his life, was heard at length. He expressed sorrow that Mrs. Hutchinson had made a comparison between his preaching and that of his brother ministers, but when asked whether he had heard her criticize them as "not able ministers," he replied that he "did not remember" hearing her say that. Reminded by Hugh Peter that "She spake plump that we were not sealed," he still persisted that he "did not remember," repeating his denial several times.

This negative testimony might have saved Mrs. Hutchinson, for Cotton's word (without oath) was not challenged, but at just this point Mrs. Hutchinson did not hold her tongue. Instead, she ended all hope of her release by offering to give her grounds for determining a right ministry and a wrong one. In her own conscience she asserted that she knew the truth.

"How do you know?" asked Mr. Nowell.

"How did Abraham know that it was God that had bid him to offer his son?" she answered.

"By an individual voice," said Deputy Governor Dudley.

"Yes, so to me by an immediate revelation. By the voice of his own spirit [God's] to my soul." She went even further. "But now having seen him which is invisible, I fear not what man can do unto me."

"Daniel was delivered by miracle," Governor Winthrop added.

"Do you think to be deliver'd so too?"

"Yes," she answered. "I do here speak it before this court. I look that the Lord should deliver me by his providence."

She had condemned herself. Winthrop was ready with his answer. "A providence of God hath answered our desires and made her to lay open herself and the ground of all these disturbances to be by revelations. This is the thing that hath been the root of all the mischief."

"We all consent with you," said the Court.

Once again John Cotton was put on the anxious seat. "Do you witness for her or against her?" he was asked. In vain he strove to save himself from a direct answer and also to save the victim. There was a difference between two kinds of revelation, he began, one in the scriptural sense which is natural, and one which implies a miracle.

"Sir, you weary me and do not satisfy me," said the deputy governor. "Do you approve of her revelations?"

"I know not whether I understand her," Cotton answered, and then marked out very carefully the safe revelation for her to choose. God might save her in a way of Providence in the scriptural sense, but not by a miracle. She did not take the hint. Perhaps she did not understand him.

The Court desired to force a reply from Cotton as to whether he did or did not witness for her, but John Winthrop reminded them that Anne Hutchinson was the one being tried, not John Cotton. The three ministers who were to witness against her were then called. Speaking under oath and reading from his notes, John Eliot repeated her statement that except for John Cotton and John Wheelwright, all the ministers of the colony (including the three under oath) were not able ministers. They were "not sealed." "I do remember, I have it in writing therefore I do avouch it." He continued. "The question being asked whether there was a difference between Mr. Cotton and us, she said there was a broad difference. I would not stick upon words — the thing she said — and that Mr. Cotton did preach a covenant of grace and we of works and she gave this reason — to put a work in evidence is a revealing upon a work. We did labour then to convince her that our doctrine was the same with Mr.

Cotton's: she said no, for we were not sealed. This is all I shall say." [6]

Pastor Welde, in response to a question from the chair, replied, "Yes, she had said that." This testimony brought the case back to the charge Governor Winthrop had announced at the beginning of the session.

"The case is altered," he announced, "and will not stand with us now, but I see a marvelous providence of God to bring things to pass as they are . . . I am persuaded that the revelation she brings forth is delusion."

All the Court and all but two or three of the ministers cried out, "We all believe it. We all believe it." Governor Winthrop rose. "The court hath already declared themselves satisfied concerning the things you hear, and concerning the troublesomeness of her spirit and the danger of her course amongst us, which is not to be suffered. Therefore if it be the mind of the court that Mistress Hutchinson for these things that appear before us is unfit for our society, and if it be the mind of the court that she shall be banished out of our liberties and imprisoned untill she be sent away, let them hold up their hands."

All but three did so.

"Those that are contrary minded hold up yours."

Only two responded in the negative, Mr. Coddington and Mr. Colburn.

> Governor: "Mistress Hutchinson, the sentence of the court you hear is that you are banished out of our jurisdiction as being a woman not fit for our society, and are to be imprisoned until the court send you away."

> Mrs. Hutchinson: "I desire to know wherefore I am banished."

Governor: "Say no more, the court knows wherefore and is satisfied."

In the colony records of Massachusetts, stating her banishment, the charge reads. "Mistress Hutchinson (the wife of William Hutchinson), being convented for traducing the mi[niste]rs, and their ministry in this country, she declared voluntarily her revelations for her ground, & that shee should bee deliv'red, & the Court ruined, with their posterity, & thereupon was banished, & the meane while was committed to Mr. Joseph Welde untill the Court shall dispose of her." [7] Through the civil power of the Court the church of Boston had gotten rid of this most troublesome member.

But the sentence of exile would not be carried out until she had also been tried before the church membership. Winter was coming on, and the church trial was postponed until spring. Separated from her husband and her family of children, she spent these months as a prisoner in Roxbury, at the home of Joseph Welde, brother of Thomas Welde, colleague pastor of John Eliot. Her solitude was broken by the coming and going of the ministers of the bay who strove to confute her errors and bring her back to orthodox belief. John Eliot, now only a few doors away, saw her often, always taking careful notes of their conversation. A desolate winter for Anne Hutchinson indeed. A proud woman, much overwrought, lonely, seeing only those who opposed her, and with spring promising only exchange of imprisonment for exile, in this four-month isolation she was a pathetic figure. She would be far less ready for the church ordeal than she had been for her civil trial, and for her this second arraignment would be the far more humiliating of the two.

John Cotton also saw her frequently during the winter. He advised confession and contrition for her errors, and a complete renouncement of them all. She consented and he helped her put her confession in order to be read before the church. Had she kept only to this statement, she might still have been saved from the verdict of excommunication, but to do so, she would have needed to be someone other than Anne Hutchinson.

On March 15, 1637/38, she was brought to the Boston meetinghouse, to be dealt with "in the church way." [8] The room was crowded to the doors with those who had listened to her in her parlor, those who had opposed her at the General Court trial and many more who had come to witness this drama in their midst. Sentiment had changed during the winter months and on this day of reckoning, a second time, she faced a company in which the majority were now hostile.

The session began with a rebuke for her tardiness, although Thomas Oliver, ruling elder of the church who was her escort, explained that the reason for being late was her physical weakness. A pale, emaciated woman stood before them, Thomas Leverett read the list of errors laid to her charge, thirty-two of them, as they had been listed by the ministers who had interviewed her during her imprisonment in Roxbury. Anne Hutchinson immediately responded by protesting that public use was being made of private conversation without her knowledge or permission. "I think it is a Breach of Church Rule," she said, "to bringe a Thinge in publike before they have dealt with me in private."

Her objection was lamely answered and she was faced with her first error. The soul is mortal.

"Yes, the soul dies; the Spirit returns to God," she replied. Her authority was two verses of Scripture in which the words *soul* and *spirit* occur. Other Scripture, also with the words soul and spirit were used to disprove her statement. No one attempted to define the words. Instead back and forth the supporting verses flew until the moderator invited those members who condemned her error to hold up their hands. They did so and the second error was read.

This one concerned the resurrection of the body. "I do not think the Body that dies shall rise again," she asserted in a firm voice.

A somewhat wandering discussion followed in many voices until John Eliot arose to speak. "We are altogether unsatisfied with her answer & we thinke it is very dangerous to dispute this Question so longe in this Congregation . . . we much feare her spirit."

Other ministers agreed. "These are Opinions that cannot be borne. They shake the very foundation of our faith," John Davenport added. There appeared to be no dissent from this view. A few moments earlier John Davenport had brought a less positive attitude into the discussion by addressing himself quietly to Anne Hutchinson in an effort to get at what was back of her apparent disbelief. She had felt his kindliness and had listened. Several times she asked for further light. "I am not clear," she said, and then patiently he tried to clarify her thinking. She was resolute in her own view, but not stubborn. Several times she asked him further questions.

For ten hours the examination went on, and at the end of the day only three of her errors had been disposed of, each time by the condemnation of her view by the church members. As the sun went down and the unlighted church grew dark, John Wilson said, "Let us refer the rest to next Lecture day. But first let us vote to admonish her." Before the vote was taken, one of her older sons interrupted. How could he vote when "mother is not convinced," he asked. John Wilson rebuked him. This was no case for maternal affection, and both sons were forthwith included in the admonition with their mother.

John Cotton gave it, beginning with her words spoken on the ship when she had come over months before. The substance of his long speech was, We received you into the church. You have done some good. But we have things against you. You have brought dishonor to God.

Midway in his list of her errors, Mrs. Hutchinson interrupted him. "All that I would say is this that *I did not hould any of thease Thinges* before my Imprisonment."

Paying no heed to this statement, Cotton went on. "Therefore I do admonish you . . ." only to be interrupted again, this time by Thomas Shepard, who "with grief," declared "she spoke of these very things when I was with her. This makes me more to fear the unsoundness of her hart than all the rest." John Eliot corroborated Shepard, and on that ominous note, John Wilson went on, "I require yow in the name of the Church to present yo'selfe hear agayne next Lecture day to answer to such other things as we charge you with."

During the ensuing week she was left at John Cotton's house in imprisonment. On March 22, she again appeared before the same company, was faced with the remaining errors, acknowledged them all and stated that she now saw more clearly. Then as though triumphantly, John Wilson announced that there was one more thing necessary for her to answer. That was her remark at the close of the preceding session when she had said that she held none of the errors charged against her prior to her imprisonment. Thomas Shepard says that you spoke of them to him.

"I spoke rashly," she replied. "I do not slight any man. If Mr. Shepard doth conceave that I had any of these Thinges in my mind, then he is deceaved."

"If she says others are mistaken," Shepard answered, "I fear it will not stand with true Repentance."

John Eliot agreed that Shepard had spoken truly. Anne Hutchinson had said the same to him.

John Cotton tried to help her. Two things to be cleared, he told her. "What you do now hould and what you did hould."

"My judgment is not altered, though my expression alters," she replied.

"Most dangerous," said John Wilson and a chorus of assent followed this verdict. Deputy Governor Dudley took the floor. "Her repentance will be worse than her Errors. Her Repentance is in a paper, not in her Countenance. Let the elders say whether she held those opinions before her imprisonment." All the ministers spoke at once, agreeing that she held them prior.

"Let her speak plainly what her judgement now is," said John Eliot, but it was too late. Instead, condemnation came from every lip. There was no mercy. "A notorious impostor," said Thomas Shepard.

"I look to her as a dangerous agent of the devil," said John Wilson. "Let the church express itself if of another mind."

"It is a wonderful wisdom of God . . . to let her fall into such lies as she hath done this day," added John Eliot.

"We are bound to remove her upon the lie," said Shepard.

Mr. Scott spoke. "Were it not better to give her a little time? She is not yet convinced of her Lye."

A stranger asked whether the church proceeded against her for doctrine or for the lie. John Wilson replied that for his part, it should be for her errors in opinion. "She hath made some show of Repentance, yet it doth not seem to be cordial or sincere."

Cotton at last turned against her. "As soon as ever Annaias had told a Lye, the church cast him out," he said. That settled it. A biblical analogy was all they needed at this point.

"Thou hast not lied unto men but unto God," said John Wilson. "The Church consenting to it, we shall now proceed to excommunication." He put the motion and then spoke the dread words: "Forasmuch as yow, Mistress Hutchinson, have highly transgressed, and offended, & forasmuch as yow have soe many ways *troubled the Church* with yor Errors & have drawen away many a poor soule, & have *upheld yor Revelations;* and forasmuch as you have made a Lye &c. . . . Therefore in the name of our Lord Je[sus] Ch[rist] & in the name of the Church, I doe not only pronounce yow worthy to be cast out, but I doe *cast yow out & deliver yow up to Sathan,* that yow may learne no more to blaspheme, to seduce & to lye, & I doe account you from this time forth to be a Hethen and a Publican, & soe to be held of all the Brethren & Sisters, of this congregation, & of others; therefor *I command you in the name of Ch[rist] Je[sus]* and of this Church *as a Leper to withdraw yor selfe owt of this Congregation,* that as formerly you have despised and contemned the Holy Ordinances of God, & turned yor Backe on them, soe yow may now have no part in them nor benefit by them."

Had she heard correctly? Stunned perhaps, she turned slowly, faced her former friends and neighbors, her adherents, straightened herself up to her full height, head erect, and walked slowly, all eyes upon her, down the meetinghouse aisle. Mary Dyer, her close friend, who one day would die on Boston gallows for being a Quaker, rose from her seat and walked with her. Both women were victims of an unyielding system they had tried to break. The door closed behind them.

Records of First Church, Boston, from which she had been cast out read, "The 23rd of the 1st month, 1638, Anne, the wife of our brother, William Hutchinson, having on the 15th of this month been openly, in the public congregation, admonished of sundry errors held by her, was on the same 22nd day cast out of the church for impenitently persisting in a manifest lie, then expressed by her in open congregation."

Testimonies from many sources dismiss this unhappy chapter of Anne Hutchinson's exile and excommunication with

firm assumption that orthodoxy would henceforth be safe in
New England. "Now the churches had rest and were multi-
plied," wrote Roger Clap. They were "brought off from her
errors and settled again in the truth," wrote John Winthrop.
Nathaniel Ward's extravagant oft-quoted contribution suggests has there were those who voiced criticism of the treatment she had received.  He wrote: "I will petition to be
chosen the universal idiot of the world if all the wits under
the heavens can lay their heads together and find an assertion
worse than this that men ought to have liberty of conscience,
and that it is persecution to debar them of it."

As for Anne, a virtual prisoner in her house during the
nine days allotted to her by the Court, she packed her belong-
ings, took the nine children still at home and departed to the
Coddington colony in Rhode Island, where briefly she
thought her own thoughts and in some measure reestablished
her court. Here in 1642 her husband died. Trouble arose
and she moved again, this time to Astoria on Long Island,
later to the mainland on the shores of Pelham Bay where the
end came in her massacre and that of all her children save
little Susan.

She had left a long memory behind her in Boston, Roxbury
and neighboring towns, but after the immediate strain of the
trial days had passed, her quick departure was a relief, and
sooner than anyone might have imagined, she faded out of
the daily conversation.  But dominant conceptions changed
slowly in those days, and when word came back of her massacre her fate was generally accepted as God's judgment against
her.  Later generations have honored her as champion of freedom in religious belief, as is scarcely true. Demanding independence for herself, she was also the assailant of those who
believed differently. Freedom in religion wide enough to
permit more than one view would take longer, much longer.

Hers is a sad story, sad chiefly in its loneliness and waste. She had large capacity for religious experience and also for leadership. She lived too soon for either to be realized.

John Eliot's part in this unhappy story shows him, at the age of thirty-three, already firmly fitted into the pattern of the first-generation minister. After five years of association with Thomas Welde in Roxbury, it is too easy to say that he had allowed the elder man to be his tutor. Possibly, but by no means certainly. At this date the conservative view prevailed in the pulpit all over New England and was not determined by age. John Eliot would have been asleep for a long generation before young ministers would be dismissed from their pulpits for holding new and different opinions, and for a far longer one before they would be speaking their convictions freely.

In this early Boston religious crisis John Eliot had put himself on record as a champion of orthodoxy. His witness against Anne Hutchinson had confirmed in him loyalties that would be lifelong. It had also given him standing as a young man among the pulpit men of his generation. As orthodoxy saw it, truth had triumphed over error, and he had been one of those who had helped to bring about the victory.

## A SHARE IN NEW ENGLAND'S
## FIRST PUBLISHED BOOK

IT MAY HAVE BEEN with something of relief that back in Roxbury after the trial, John Eliot turned to another extrapulpit task, a quiet one that he could perform in his own study. This one concerned translation, and may for him have had prophetic overtones. Ministers and magistrates of the Boston region had decided that it was time for their meetinghouses to have their own version of the Psalms "fit to be sung on Sabbath," and "good Hebricians" among the clergy were invited to prepare it.

Some knowledge of John Eliot's linguistic interest and special skill must have preceded his inclusion in this scholarly group, since as one of the younger ministers, he would hardly have come forward among older men whose flair for verse was known. John Cotton, according to Cotton Mather, had "a nimble faculty of putting his Devout thoughts into Verse." John Wilson was producing enough verse to make a volume. In fact, all of the thirty ministers in the Boston region (John Eliot among them) had been trained from grammar school days in verse writing, and no one was a complete novice in meter. There is a tradition (unsubstantiated) that John Eliot in his Cambridge days had a reputation for unusual linguistic ability, but one suspects this tradition of being a mere backward glance after his translation some years later of the Bible into the Indian tongue. At any rate he is known to have been a participant in the creation of this songbook.

Evidence comes in the half-serious quatrain of Thomas Shepard:

You Roxbury Poets, keep clear of the Crime,
Of missing to give us very good Rhime,
And you of Dorchester, your verses lengthen,
But with the Texts own Words you will them strengthen.[1]

Thomas Welde and John Eliot were the Roxbury poets and Richard Mather the "you of Dorchester."

Until Mr. Zoltan Haraszti clarified our knowledge of authorship for this new psalmbook, the notion had persisted that these three men were the sole authors. We know differently now. "The Chief Divines of the Country" were the translators and versifiers whose joint labor produced it. There is also mention of Francis Quarles of England as sending over his translation of Psalms 6, 16, 25, 57, 88 and 137.[2]

As published in 1640, this book is commonly referred to as *The Bay Psalm Book,* but in its original edition of this year, it was entitled *The Whole Book of Psalms, faithfully translated into English Metre.* It was printed on the Stephen Daye Press in Cambridge in 1640. The aim had been a "plaine and familiar translation of the psalmes and words of David," the emphasis being on translation rather than paraphrase, fidelity rather than poetry. One would expect such an ideal for Puritans, and this book belonged to its time, 1640, and its place, New England. Thomas Welde later wrote in his *The Practices of the Churches in New England,* "We have endeavored, according to our light and time, to retranslate the Psalmes, as near the originall as we could, into meeter." [3] And that is precisely what these "good Hebricians" attempted to do.

The desire for a new songbook "according to our own light and time" probably owed something also to the dawning new sense that this "wilderness" was their own country. With each of the ten years just passed, the Massachusetts Bay pioneers had become increasingly aware that they were not transients in this new land, as the first explorers had been, but on the way to be possessors of it. It is "our land," they were saying, and they were using the phrases "our cornfields," "our fields and harvest," perhaps unconsciously. In many connections the word "our" was slipping into the informal bulletins sent back to the mother country. Ten years of labor had begun to confer ownership by more than legal deed. The desire for a new songbook, "our own," distinct from Sternhold and Hopkins, which they had brought with them, or Ainsworth, which was used by Plymouth, was another instance of this new spirit.

How the one hundred and fifty Psalms were parceled out among the "good Hebricians" is not recorded, nor do we know which or how many of the clergy were included. We only know that when all contributions were assembled, Thomas Shepard of Cambridge put them in shape for printing. He also, no doubt deliberately, eliminated all marks of individual authorship, giving to the whole book the style of one man. Even the six translations by Francis Quarles show no individual traits by which they can be identified. The preface, long supposed to be the work of Richard Mather, is now identified by Mr. Haraszti as written by John Cotton. Evidence for this new assignment comes from a manuscript draft preserved in the Prince collection. This draft is printed entire in the appendix to Mr. Haraszti's book.[4]

These Psalms are faithfully translated and owe much to the vocabulary of the King James Bible, which in its 1611 edition all but the oldest clergy would have used since childhood. It is well to remember in judging these verses, that a metrical version for purposes of a songbook does not necessarily promise to be poetical. How many hymns can meet a high standard as poetry?

For twentieth-century readers, now that quite different

motives are shaping translations of the Bible (sometimes frighteningly), the verses of this early songbook may seem even stranger to modern ears. Even to understand them as the conscientious work of erudite men who were trained scholars, one needs to read John Cotton's preface with strict attention and then see that the ideal he is setting forth is exemplified in any psalm to which one may apply it. For example, to the familiar ninety-first:

Psalm 91 (1st Part)

1. He that within the secret place
        of the most high doth dwell,
   he under the Almightyes shade
        shall lodge himselfe *full well.*
2. My hope, he is, & my fortresse,
        I to the Lord will say:
   he is my God; & I in him
        my confidence will stay.
3. Surely out of the fowlers snare
        he shall deliver thee,
   also thee from the Pestilence
        infectious shall free,
4. He with his feathers hide thee shall,
        under his wings shall bee
   thy trust: his truth shall be a shield
        and buckler unto thee.
5. Thou shalt not be dismaide with feare
        for terrour by the night:
   nor for the arrow that with speed
        flyeth in the day light:
6. Nor for the Pestilence that doth
        walk in the darkness fast:
   nor for the sore destruction
        that doth at noone day wast.[5]

Naturally, as more than three centuries have gone by since 1640, this first book to be published in America has greatly increased in value, both for collectors of Americana and for students of early American culture. The last copy offered for sale in 1947 was purchased for $150,000.00, the highest price ever paid for an American book. Only eleven extant copies are known, all but one of these owned by American libraries.

Even in its own far-distant day, this was a relatively rare book, though for very different reasons. It was probably owned by only a few members of the church in the town and was perhaps the only book besides the Bible on the family shelf. It belongs to its own day almost completely, and to be fairly judged must be kept within that framework of thought and life. By intent as bare of ornament as the unplastered, unpainted and perhaps unfloored little meetinghouse, it is a deeply revealing document of early American values for living.

To be judged fairly, also, it should be *heard*, not *read*, for this is a singing book. Lined out by the precentor and then sung, without instrument, by every worshiper on the benches, it afforded a release to the spirit and, possibly also as they sang together, they experienced something of what the phrase "communion of saints" might suggest.

How did it sound? Perhaps melodious enough to merit the verdict beautiful, or certainly tuneful, depending on the ear and voice of the precentor, as he arose from his seat directly in front of the pulpit and led the congregation in their half hour of praise. He would have been chosen as leader because his voice was powerful and also for his ability to find the key without instrument, for the 1630's were too early even for a pitchpipe. Usually he was one of the older worshipers.

The psalm was sung antiphonally. Sometimes the precentor, after "setting the tune," intoned each line separately, the congregation repeating it after him. Sometimes he read two lines, sang the first and they replied with the second. Sometimes he sang the whole line and they replied with the second half of it only. Sometimes he sang each line in turn through the stanza and they used the first line as a refrain throughout. There were other ways, all of them using response. The result would have been spontaneous and full-throated. Contrary to a notion oft-repeated, early Puritans were well accustomed to singing. They sang psalms daily in their homes and knew words and tune without formal instruction or a book in the hand. It would be fully two generations before a widespread ignorance of music would lead to the slovenly congregational singing which brought about the great "Singing Quarrel" of the early eighteenth century. There were as yet no such "Slidings and Purrings," "Little Flourishes of the Voice," individual "Turns and Quavers," which in the words of one critic made "an Ungrateful Jarr in the Ears of those who can well distinguish Sounds." The time was still two lifetimes away before choirs would be born or the "Devil's Fiddle" be brought into the meetinghouse.

To John Eliot's far earlier generation, who were still not far removed from the Elizabethan tradition of music, the publication of *The Bay Psalm Book* was an event in which they took pride. To have been one of the creators of this small volume was a shared honor, but an honor for John Eliot. It made an important page in his story as the new decade came in.

## "THE PRINCIPALL END
## OF OUR PLANTATION"

Long before the beginning of the 1640's John Eliot had found not only the direction in which he would travel zestfully for the remainder of his life, but also the field on which he would build something to form a nation's character for centuries to come. Best of all, he never knew that he had done so. Before he died, in addition to his parish duties, the specific work that he had labored to accomplish was already falling in pieces and would be written down by many as failure, but in longer perspective his permanent achievement does not lie in its literal continuance. In fact, there is no specific likeness between what he did day after day for a few hundred Indians and the deposit this early missionary service has left in the American heritage. It endures; hence America's chief reason for remembering John Eliot belongs to this chapter of the colonial story.

No mystery attaches to its beginning. Indians were often on Roxbury streets, as in most other New England towns, and settlers soon took their occasional visits for granted. Something to sell, something to buy, brief exchange in half-understood pidgin English or pidgin Algonquian phrases, not quite friendship, not conscious fear on either side; mere acceptance. Indians were part of the picture. They were also, thanks to the figure with outstretched arms on the Massachusetts colony seal, something of an obligation, at least to the ministry. In these earlier years, young men of the pulpit could not quite forget or ignore this Macedonian cry, whatever they may have thought individually of Indians at their door. In fact, when he was asked years later what had sparked his own missionary impulse toward them, John Eliot replied, first, the colony seal,[1] which he called the "public engagement," and privately, his own "pity for the poor Indian." If there were a particular circumstance which turned his pity into a consuming purpose, as is perhaps likely, he did not mention it. Perhaps he did not know what it was. His pity was for the savage in his spiritual darkness, pity for his lost soul, capable of salvation, as John Eliot fervently believed. He did not see him as being conceived as the very "dregs of humanity." This disparaging phrase came early, gained currency and may be found scores of times in sermons and other writings of the clergy. It suggests a far different attitude from John Eliot's "pity." To him the Indian was a human being, created in God's image, but "lost." He must be found, and it must be the Christian white man who gave him this chance.

Back of these two opposed views of Indians was a long history. In fact, it had begun with the discovery of America. When Columbus returned to Spain after his first voyage, he took with him nine Indians from the island of Hispaniola (Haiti) on which he had landed. Strange frightening creatures they seemed, as men of the Spanish homeland first viewed them. Were they lost souls in whom God's image was marred, or mere beasts with no capacity to know God? Whichever they might be, they were amazingly strong, and before long, Spanish plantation masters knew they could use that strength.

One year later, 1493, Pope Alexander VI issued a bull pronouncing the Indians capable of embracing the Catholic faith. Columbus himself believed this to be true even before the Pope gave it the sanction of the Church.

In his famous letter, addressed to Raphael Saixis, treasurer of Ferdinand, Columbus reported "many beautiful and pleasing things" given to the Indians on the island he called Juana, "in order that I might the more easily make them friendly to me, that they might be made worshippers of Christ." In the hope of universal Christendom with which his letter ends, he wrote, "Let Christ rejoice on earth, as he rejoices in heaven, when he foresees coming to salvation so many souls of people hitherto lost." [2]

From his second voyage we are told that Columbus brought back a "considerable number" of Indians designed for slave labor. They were sold in payment for cargoes needed in the islands. When Queen Isabella, to whom the Pope had granted power over church affairs, heard of this sale, she immediately decreed that those seized for enslavement be released; those taken as prisoners of war might be kept. But Queen Isabella died in 1504, and long before that date Spanish masters had no intention of giving up this new source of slave labor. Both the papal bull and the Queen's edict were grossly ignored and openly disobeyed.

Already, however, the Indians had a champion. He was Bartolomé de las Casas, son of a man employed by Columbus since his 1492 voyage. In 1498, six years later, young Bartolomé accompanied his father on the voyage of that year. Columbus liked the young man, and on his return gave him a native boy as his personal servant. When Queen Isabella heard of this gift, she ordered the slave set free, but the association of the two young men had been long enough for Las Casas to know personally one of the race to which he would dedicate his life.[3] One of the great controversies of the early Renaissance concerning human freedom, which culminated in a debate that echoed all over Europe, stemmed from this association.

Las Casas took the church path toward his goal. In 1502 he returned to San Domingo, was ordained priest in 1510 and thereby became the first ecclesiastic in the West Indies. Henceforth, he devoted himself exclusively to the Indians. He had great gifts which fitted him for this service: a personality which invited the confidence of the Indians, sympathy, practical friendliness and a magnetic ability to communicate with them. He became a power in their midst. As he witnessed the cruelties of his Spanish countrymen against them, his zeal increased at their defiance of royal orders, but Queen Isabella was gone and there was no authority behind the championship of a priest. His militant antagonism toward the oppressive landholders availed nothing to mitigate their cruelty. It increased, but Las Casas labored on. By his daily ministry he earned for himself the title "Apostle to the Indians," and by his public advocacy of their cause he earned another, "Protector of the Indians."

When Charles V came to the throne in 1516 and as Charles I ruled over Spain, Las Casas resolutely continued his efforts both in Spain and in the Indies. He appealed to his countrymen for justice on behalf of the Indians and cessation of the cruelties they suffered, but his appeals had little effect either in the homeland or on the islands. By that time the system of slavery had become firmly fixed and plantation owners had no intention either of giving it up or of improving the conditions under which the slaves worked. The royal government at home had no comprehension of the human suffering that went on under this system, and the citizen was not even interested. The West Indies were too far away.

For a decade Las Casas went back and forth from the islands to Spain, making one plea after another. In 1520 he tried new tactics, organizing an Indian colony in Cumana and trying single-handedly to work out an experiment in civiliza-

tion. The plan was foredoomed. In spite of detailed organization, consecration and amazing patience, no Utopia resulted. Such a project takes generations, not years.

After fourteen voyages between Spain and the West Indies,
Las Casas returned home for the last time. He was seventy-
three years old and had nineteen more years to live. Then
came the great debate at the Spanish court which put his
name in memory for generations to come. His chief antago-
nist was Juan Ginés de Sepúlveda, historian and scholar,
deeply versed in Aristotelian thought. He was a man with
large interests in the West Indies, although he had never set
foot there. "God has deprived him of any knowledge of the
New World," Las Casas asserted. As to personal observation
and experience, this statement was entirely true, but Sepúlveda was a man whom such a gibe could not even touch.

There was also Gonzalo Fernandez de Oviedo y Valdés, official historian of the West Indies, whose book Las Casas had
the boldness to declare contained as many lies as pages. He
too had large interests in the islands. These men were formidable opponents, and both had a large and sympathetic following. Occasion for the debate was the refusal of the Royal
Council to publish Sepúlveda's book, holding that it was un-
sound. Sepúlveda immediately sent it to Rome to be published in spite of the Council's verdict. Las Casas then decided
to refute it and a public debate was arranged at the court then
meeting at Valladolid. It lasted for five days, was listened to
with tense emotions on both sides, aroused bitter antagonisms
as well as extravagant praise, was quoted and discussed all over
Europe for many months, has been recalled again and again
and would be timely if recalled at the present moment.

The specific issue to which the disputants spoke concerned
the lawfulness of a Spanish war waged against the Indians before the faith had been preached to them. Should they first be

made subject to the king's rule, so that afterwards they may more easily be instructed in the faith?

The arguments against which Las Casas contended were all built on the premise that Indians were savages, being without knowledge of God or the use of reason. Therefore, Sepúlveda argued, the Spaniards by virtue of their superior wisdom and prudence were justified in making war against them. In case the Indians refused to submit, the Spaniards might force them into slavery and take their possessions. Once they had been thoroughly subdued, the argument went on, they would become docile, renounce their errors and be in condition to receive the Gospel. In a word, conquer and then convert. The superiority of the Spaniards would not make their subjugation tyrannical. Instead, it was in the Indians' interest. In such a case war is not only justifiable; it is necessary. The premise behind all this is essentially Aristotelian. The arguments Las Casas used against it were based on foundations already regarded as obsolete: the papal bull of Alexander VI and the decree of Queen Isabella against enslaving Indians. The barriers to his success were well nigh insurmountable.

Nevertheless, against Sepúlveda's dark picture of the Indian as barbarous and cruel, enormously wicked, grossly ignorant, Las Casas began by placing an equally extravagant opposing view, his own warm sympathy obscuring the darker aspects of the problem. He brushed aside his opponent's structure of conclusions, ignored the fact that thousands of Indians had been enmeshed in a system of slavery for half a century and stated as his major premise that they were essentially rational beings. As he saw it, mankind is one, and in a noble parallel to the first of America's "self-evident truths," he made it the foundation of his plea, as he had written it in his *Historia Apologética de las Indias* years before.

Thus mankind is one, and all men are alike in that which concerns their creation and all natural things, and no one is born enlightened. From this it follows that all of us must be guided and aided at first by those who were born before us. And the savage peoples of the earth may be compared to uncultivated soil that readily brings forth weeds and useless thorns, but has within itself such natural virtue that by labour and cultivation it may be able to yield sound and beneficial fruits.[4]

Then from his fifty years of association with the Indians of the Indies he set about to prove this conviction to be sound truth. He presented them as faithful, submissive and not quarrelsome if humanely treated, lacking only in knowledge of the true God to make them blessed in this world. To subdue them by war and force them to accept Christianity was not only unchristian, but it would not work. Instruction must come before baptism. War is utterly unjust and will bring obstacles to conversion that can never be surmounted. All of Las Casas' five-day argument is written in his book *Historia Apologética de las Indias,* which had been the work of years. His fervor stirred the court audience, and ineffectual though his arguments were in accomplishing immediate reform, his indictment of human slavery remained a challenge for generations to come.

A fair sample of his impassioned style comes in his concluding words to Sepúlveda, as he painted the dangers and loss to Castile and Leon, in fact to the whole of Spain, because of royal indifference to what was now going on in the islands. The desolation would be so monstrous that,

the blind may see it, the deaf hear it, the dumbe rehearse it. I invoke all the hierarchies and choirs of angels, all the saints of the celestial court, all inhabitants of the globe for witnesses that I free my conscience of all that has transpired . . . If his

Majesty leaves to Spaniards the tyranny of the government
of the Indies, all of them will be destroyed. God will punish
you. So may it be.[5]

To all of this Sepúlveda had only denials, more passionately
asserted. He knew full well what was at stake. If the Indians
were not cannibals, as he had insisted, not irrational creatures, not incapable of reason, then their lands could not be
taken away from them. If they could not be enslaved and
forced to do the work that was making Spanish manufactures
and commerce prosper, then that prosperity was gone.
Against this materialistic background, and ignoring the theological issue, he proposed the practical, almost desperate question: How can savages live as free subjects of the great
king?

The debate was over. It had settled nothing, but it had left
a new point of view echoing all over Europe. A decision as to
who had won was never formally announced. The fourteen
judges had deliberated for days, and if they reported a verdict,
it was not made public. Las Casas did not return to the Indies, but lived out his remaining days in the homeland, energetic and active until his ninety-second year.

For a later generation the parallels between him and John
Eliot catch the imagination. The two men would have
understood each other. Both believed the Indian capable of
civilization according to the Christian ideal and tradition,
and both gave the largest measure of their lifetime thought
and activity to help in bringing this to pass. Both men
preached and experimented with forming Indian towns and
colonies to that end. Through the efforts of half a century
both men earned the title "Apostle to the Indians." That
John Eliot knew of the work and writings of Las Casas is a fair
assumption, in spite of scant evidence in his writings. John
Eliot did not read Spanish, and even in translation the words

of a Spanish Catholic priest might receive slight hospitality in England after the defeat of the Spanish Armada. Richard Hakluyt, however, had printed a summary of this debate, and Elizabethan England read no one more avidly than Hakluyt.[6] One remembers also that ideas set loose in the world can be potent without quotation marks, and by the time John Eliot's generation were university students, the attitudes and ideas underneath this earlier championship of the Indian and plea for his human rights had full time to become almost anonymous. Better so. The deposit Las Casas had left in the conscience of thinking Europe had become part of the English inheritance and was still quietly at work. The presence of Indians in English seaport towns and on the streets of every New England town would again raise the questions: What is a savage? What is he capable of becoming?

As the reality of a new continent slowly dawned on the European consciousness, Indians became one of its front-line interests. Long before 1600 and increasingly thereafter, no English reader needed to be ignorant of their appearance, their habits, their customs in peace and war. Thomas Hariot's *Briefe and True Report* in 1588 had begun a long succession of detailed descriptions of their manners, their family and tribal ways. The designs of John White, engraved by De Bry, had pictured Indians in many attitudes and situations. Almost every exploring expedition brought back a small number of natives so that citizens of London, Bristol, Plymouth and other coast towns had seen them in the flesh, even decked out in paint and feathers. In a religious age it was natural to ask, Can such creatures be Christianized? The question was asked, answered and discussed many score of times.

In Elizabethan days the Christianization of the Indians was not only a religious hope, but had a relation to the glory of England. That too was natural. Religion had been one of the motivating forces in the defeat of the Spanish Armada, and with Protestantism at least temporarily the victor, after a long tension, English zeal to enlarge its territory followed. The triumphs of exploration and the first faint successes of colonization were given a religious interpretation. Rivalry with Spain for the souls of the Indian became almost militant. Examples multiply. When Sir Humphrey Gilbert landed at St. John's harbor, Newfoundland, in 1583, his first act was to announce to the startled natives that religious worship would be according to the Church of England.

"Shame it is," declared William Symonds, in a sermon before the Adventurers and Planters for Virginia, at White-chapel on April 20, 1609, "that the Jesuites and Friers, that accompany every ship, should be so diligent to destroy souls, and wee not seeke the tender lambes, nor bind up that which is broken." [7]

Robert Gay, in his *A Good Speed to Virginia* a week later, April 28, 1609, also spoke a preachment echoed many times over. "Farre be it from the hearts of the English, they should give any cause to the world, to say that they sought the wealth of that Countrie above or before the glorie of God and the propagation of his Kingdome." [8]

Under persistent propaganda from the pulpit, which was enjoying an authority seldom known before and never since those years, the conversion of the heathen became a leading motive in western expansion. Explorers and early colonists each in their turn, felt themselves part of the divine plan for the New World. Their pious phrase, "for the glory of God," was not entirely conventional, nor was there a clear line between the glory of God and the glory of England. Preacher after preacher linked them together in hopeful prophecy. Daniel Price, chaplain to Prince Henry, in a sermon at Paul's Cross, May 28, 1609, dared to say, "You will make . . . a sav-

age country to become a sanctified country; you will obtain
the saving of their souls, you will enlarge the bounds of this
kingdom, nay the bounds of Heaven, and all the angells that
behold this if they rejoice so much at the conversion of one
sinner, O what will be their joy at the conversion of so
many." [9]

No wonder seamen and adventurers thought of themselves
as carrying the Gospel to the utmost ends of the earth. That
materialistic concerns might profit from the religious motive
was completely understandable in view of such preaching.
Spread the Gospel and you will be prosperous became a frequent theme.

Religion was, of course, a part of shipboard life and usually
there was a chaplain to take charge of some form of daily worship. If not, there was worship without him. The picture of
Sir Francis Drake and his men after landing on the Pacific
coast, on their knees, praying, singing and pointing upward
to suggest to their Indian spectators that they worshiped the
God of heaven is completely typical.[10] This was the first time
these far-western Indians had heard Protestant prayers and
psalms. They understood nothing of the lay sermon by the
great captain, but they liked the singing and asked for more.
We may not call Sir Francis Drake a religious man, but he
was a militant Protestant. He had brought about the defeat
of the Spanish Armada, and in his thought and that of thousands of Englishmen of his day hatred of Catholicism could
not be separated from English patriotism. The combination
had spelled a magnificent victory.

After colonization began in 1607, the challenge to Chris-
tianize the savages became more precise. One finds it in official and informal correspondence almost whenever the New
World was the subject. King James' letter to Sir Thomas
Gates is typical.

We greatly commending, and graciously accepting of their
desire for the furtherance of so noble a work, which may by
the providence of Almighty God hereafter tend to the glory
of his divine Majesty, in propagating of Christian religion to
such people as yet live in darkness and miserable ignorance
of the true knowledge and worship of God, and may in time
bring the infidels and savages living in these parts, to human
civility, and to a settled and quiet government; Do by these
my letters patent, graciously accept of, and agree to, their
humble and well intended desires.[11]

In many sermons, prospective colonists were enjoined in
words that would presently be part of their charter grants,
"Only *let your principal end be the propagation of the glorious Gospel,*" said John Donne in 1622, "not gaine, nor glory,
but to gaine Soules to the glory of God; this Seals the great
Seal, this justifies Justice itself, this authorises Authority, and
gives power strength to itselfe." [12]

In the letter of Matthew Craddock, Governor of the Company to Governor Endicott, February 16, 1629, these words,
"We trust you will not be unmindfull of the main end of our
Plantation, by endeavouring to bring the Indians to the
knowledge of the Gospel." [13]

The King's grant to the Council of Plymouth keeps these
same pulpit phrases, "the principall effect which I can desire
or expect of this action is the conversion of the people of these
parts unto the true worship of God and Christian religion." [14]

The charter of Massachusetts Bay pledged the colony "to
wynn and incite the natives of [the] country to the knowledge
and obedience of the onlie true God and Savior of mankinde,
and the Christian faythe [was in the] royall intention and the
adventurers' free profession, the principall ende of this plantation." [15]

Oaths administered to the Governor and Deputy Governor

bound them to "do [their] best endeavo$^r$ to draw on the natives of this country, called New England, to the knowledge of the true God." As a perpetual reminder of this obligation, the seal of the colony was devised to show the Indian with outstretched arms crying, "Come over and help us." After many years this pictured appeal would become too familiar any longer to keep officials or citizenry in remembrance of this central obligation, but that would be a long time from the beginning. For more than a century and a half every election sermon would also be a fresh reminder.

In addition to the charter obligation, there was in early days also a fairly widespread notion that the Indians had originally belonged to one of the tribes of ancient Israel, and "if they be Jewes, they must not be neglected." Proof that they were Jews consisted in a long series of resemblances that to a modern reader seem almost incredibly casual as the work of the scholars who selected them and wrote books to prove them valid. The least suggestion of similarity was accepted as evidence. The resemblances listed by Thomas Thorowgood in his *Jewes in America or Probabilities that the Americans are Jewes,* lists among his First Conjecture the Indian assumption that "their ancestors came from the southwest, and thither they all goe dying." His Second Conjecture includes similarities in Indian rites, ceremonies and opinions to those of the Jews. An astounding variety they are: Indians anoint their heads, wear earrings, delight in dancing, weep much, wash stranger's feet, compute time by nights, mothers nurse their children, messengers run with speed, a widow marries the brother of her deceased husband. Among sacred rites, beliefs and customs he lists circumcision, knowledge of the flood, belief in immortality, the building of their temples foursquare, belief that the world will end, that the body will rise from the dead, the custom of offering the first fruits to deity. Under his Third Conjecture concerning words and manner of speech, he finds that they say *Hallelujah*. How could they have heard this from any Christian?

The exhibit of such details as proof apparently satisfied Hebraic scholars of Thomas Thorowgood's generation, some of whom also worried themselves to try to determine which of the Ten Tribes was honored to be the ancestor of the American Indians and also to discover how these first wanderers could have found their way here. Even greater ingenuity was required to explain this marvel. America must once have been bound to Asia. Time and the sea have made the gap wider. Around Florida "the land runs out large toward the north." This might have been the place where they crossed over. Those of another school of cosmology argued for the far-northern route around Greenland. Late in the century credibility lessened, but did not disappear, and the game was engaging while it lasted.

John Eliot was too practical a man to be long detained by these arguments and too sure of his own commission from God to find a missionary motive in them, but Thomas Thorowgood was an acquaintance, and when he invited John Eliot to write a brief discourse for the second edition of *Jewes in America* (1660), he complied, going as far as to say, "I thought I saw some ground to conceive, that some of the Ten Tribes might be scattered that far, into these parts of America." [16] Truly the Bible says, he went on, that the Ark landed "eastward of the land of Eden, and if so, then surely into America, because that is part of the eastern world. Hence why ought we not to believe a portion of the Ten tribes landed in America."

Clearly Eliot derived no convictions from these arguments. In the twenty-two pages he supplied to the second edition, he was paying a courtesy to a friendly acquaintance who had in-

terested several Englishmen in the Indian towns John Eliot
was building at the time. These frail speculations did not be-
long to his world. John Cotton attempted to prove from the
Apocalypse that the conversion of the "heathen" must wait
upon the "coming in of the Jews." Roger Williams also
bowed to this opinion, although he did not delay his preaching to the Indians upon that contingency. Other first-
generation ministers, as well as an occasional layman, Samuel
Sewall, for example, gave time and thought to these vague
possibilities, but to John Eliot, the "Poor Indian" at his door
was argument enough, and he went to work.

It would not be easy. The Indians of New England were
not saying, "Come over and help us," as the seal of Massachusetts announced. In fact, they had never said it. Ever since
the coming of the earliest explorers, the summer fishermen,
the first Plymouth and Boston settlers, Indians had responded
to Englishmen with guarded friendliness, usually with a tinc-
ture of suspicion, or half-concealed ill will. The Indian had
learned some useful things from the white man, and he had
often been a helpful teacher in return. Each side had taken
life of the other. Now and then an Indian had wandered into
the meetinghouse on Sunday and had heard what he did not
understand. Communication between the races was still hes-
itant and stumbling. By 1640 they were still aliens in feeling,
and in civilization they were centuries and continents apart.
Missionary work among them had already begun under the
Mayhew family on the Cape. Roger Williams had preached
to them in their own language at Plymouth and Providence,
but otherwise John Eliot faced an almost completely unplowed field. As missionary to the red man he was one of the
first pioneers in New England, and the key to whatever success he would have was deeply personal. He went to them as a
friend, and the bridge was crossed.

## CHALLENGE OF
## THE ALGONQUIAN LANGUAGE

INDIANS AT Roxbury doors were of the Massachusetts tribe which once had many encampments in the region of the Bay. They had been a numerous and great people, whose population was estimated in many thousands, but shortly before the coming of the Plymouth settlers in 1620, vast numbers of them had been swept away by a great plague or some other "epidemicall sickness." This had been God's way of "clearing the land" for "his people" of the English settlement, John Cotton had told the vanguard of John Winthrop's company in his farewell sermon to them in 1630. For years every pulpit in New England repeated this great favor of God to his chosen people. The tract, *New England's First Fruits,* put it in print in 1643, among what "the good hand of God" has done for us, "In sweeping away great multitudes of natives by the small pox, a little before we went thither, that he might make room for us there." [1]

John Winthrop, writing to Nathaniel Rich in the same year had said, "the natives are neare all dead of the small Poxe, so as the Lord hathe cleared our title to what we possess." Apparently this second outbreak was also a favor to the whites in the destruction of their red brothers. Even so, the Massachusetts Indians still numbered thousands until after King Philip's War, more than a generation away.

These Indians belonged to the Algonquian language group, whose speech in spite of various dialectical peculiarities of neighboring tribes, was also understood by the Wampanoags of the Cape region, the Narragansets farther south in Plymouth colony, the Pequots most southerly of all. Within the large territory of the four New England colonies, Plymouth, Massachusetts Bay, Connecticut and Rhode Island, there were also many other smaller Indian tribes belonging to this same language group, Nipmucks, Mohegans, Cape Cods, Pocumtucks and various others.

Had there been strong unity among these numerous Indian groups, an earlier peril than King Philip's War might have completely wiped out the English settlements, but these tribes were enmeshed in mutual hatreds generations long. They had fought a succession of wars against each other past the memory of any but the oldest of the tribe, and despite their resentment of English encroachment, they would have needed a far more magnetic leader than Philip proved to be in order to bring about a concerted action against the English in the early days. During this period bitter grievances accumulated. Inevitably, a general Indian war against the English would come, and it would be battle to the death. Even as early as 1640 the signs pointing to it were unmistakable, but one after another they were brushed aside. Maybe it won't come, the English said, and in fact, there were forty years of uneasy peace before war broke out.

John Eliot's labors for the conversion of the Indians belonged to this troubled period. Inevitably also, his missionary labors contributed to the unrest between Indian and white man. Tribal chiefs lost something of the loyalty of his Praying Indians who lived in their own towns and had scant dealing with others of their tribe. White traders also lost something of their revenue when the Praying Indians learned new skills which made them able to supply most of their own needs. Most of the New England clergy were sympathetic to John Eliot's missionary labors, but large numbers of laymen in the churches were strongly skeptical. First ardors had cooled. Indians were viewed more realistically by white settlers. It was now quite generally recognized that they were not imploring the English to show them the way to salvation. After ten years of residence, the English were too busy, too deeply involved in making their new situation safe and prosperous, educating their children, building new towns, for the Christianization of the Indians to be "the principal end of our plantation," as they had once alleged. The singleness and sense of obligation of the earlier contract could not be restored. Many also doubted the soundness of Indian conversions, and as suspicion of Indians deepened after the mid-century, there was a growing unwillingness to trust a Praying Indian in his alleged loyalty to the English.

There is no doubt that John Eliot was aware of these cross currents of indifference, even ill will and open opposition to his efforts, but from first to last, he acted as though they did not exist. He knew that a comfortably large body of church members were behind him, and that throughout the country there would be a sense of relief that at last New England was fulfilling her charter obligation. He envisioned the successful Christianization of the entire Indian population and went about his preaching to that end as a man blind to whatever stood in his way.

The immediate barrier, as he well knew, was the Algonquian language. In order to be understood, sermons must be preached in the native tongue of the Indians. Otherwise a preacher might as well not open his mouth. Thoughtful men of both clergy and laity had recognized this for a long time. Thomas Lechford, lawyer, Henry Dunster, president of Harvard, had spoken out plainly. Roger Williams could debate with the Indians in their own tongue, the Mayhews on Martha's Vineyard were preaching in it, but the discipline was too formidable, and young men hospitable to missionary work hesitated to undergo its rigors. John Eliot faced them squarely. His persistence in spite of difficulty was impressive, perhaps more so than any other of his personal qualities. When possessed by a conviction, he was driven by a zeal nothing could break. That "painful yet unwearied Minister of the Gospel" one of his colleagues called him, and the epithet fits him perhaps more neatly than any other that could be devised. Furnished with this resource and with the blessing of many friends behind him, he began his more than forty-year missionary campaign with many things in his favor.

From the beginning of his New England residence, he had been talking with Indians, and with his flair for language, in ten years he had probably learned enough of everyday Indian speech not only to understand and be understood in the small give and take his Roxbury residence demanded, but also to speak with ease and perhaps some fluency of more than buying and selling, food, raiment, and the perils of strong drink. But to preach to Indians would be quite another matter.

We do not know precisely when or under what compulsions he decided to master the language as a scholar, but from his own statement we know that his first Indian instructor was "a pregnant-witted young Indian" who had been captured during the Pequot War while on a visit to Massachusetts. He has been identified as Cockenoe of Long Island, who was working as a household servant in the home of Richard Collicot of Dorchester, a sergeant in the New England army, and very probably the captor of this Indian boy. While in service here, Cockenoe learned to speak English fluently, but he did not know how to write. John Eliot heard of his fluency and employed him. "He was the first that I made use of to teach me words, and to be my interpreter," [2] Eliot wrote.

To a linguistic scholar, even one skilled in Greek and Latin and also a deep student of Hebrew, the difficulties with the Algonquian language could hardly have been more perplexing. The language had no written texts, no dictionary, no grammar. There was not a printed word in existence, only the strange, guttural syllables and stranger rhythms, totally unlike those of European languages. John Eliot's trained ear recognized the clarity of Cockenoe's speech in which these guttural sounds gave the impression of words. Had his young teacher been able to write these sounds phonetically, the older pupil's difficulties would have been greatly lessened, but Cockenoe was at first helpless with a pencil. Clarity of speech was initially more important, however, as another trained linguist, Roger Williams, would write in his *Key to the Indian Language*. "The life of language is in the Pronunciation," [3] and John Eliot presumably recognized the truth of this observation. Roger Williams' book was not yet in print, but it is quite possible the two men had talked.

As John Eliot listened to Cockenoe's clear pronunciation, he carefully wrote down the words as they sounded, dividing them into syllables. Most carefully he noted the endings. The Algonquian language is heavily inflected, so that after hundreds of words with the same ending had been noted, the trained scholar would begin to have some clue to the relationship of these words to other words in the sentence unit. Strange phenomena began to appear. This is a language in which relationships are expressed by compounds, not by connecting units of speech such as prepositions and conjunctions. Words of enormous length are made up of syllables that appear in other words of amazing length, but with these syllables differently distributed. The student of ancient language has met with this phenomenon before and knows what to watch for in order to unthread the maze. Nouns in European languages are masculine and feminine, but after hundreds of

Algonquian nouns have been studied, the distinction is found to be animate and inanimate. Animate nouns make a plural in *og;* inanimate in *ash*. To discover this law, the student needs more than a good ear. He must have a sense of language behavior different from that of his own native speech. This sense John Eliot possessed.

One discovery led to another. Where is the verb substantive, *is, was, am, are?* After long search the conclusion comes that there is no verb substantive in Algonquian. Then the search begins for a substitute. To the trained linguist, such discoveries are exciting and rewarding, and each confers power toward another, but even so, the time, the patience, the discipline required is exhausting merely to think about.

He reported his method of work, showing him not only capable of the needed discipline, but also of finding the way toward mastery. "I diligently marked the difference of their grammar from ours; when I found the way of them, I would pursue a word, a noun, a verb through all variations I could think of. And thus I came at it." [4]

Years later he wrote a grammar of the Algonquian, calling it "Some Bones and Ribs preparatory to a Grammar," and in reading it, one may feel something of the thrill of discovery on nearly every page. It is an exciting book. Linguists who found it a century later marveled at the intuition with which this much earlier scholar had come at the laws of a savage language, without helps of any kind. One of them, Peter du Ponceau, wrote in 1832 this tribute, "The great and good man . . . did not foresee, when he wrote his Indian Grammar, that it would be sought after and studied by the learned of all nations, as a powerful help towards the improvement of a science not then in existence; I mean the Comparative Science of Languages." [5]

Linguist as he was, however, John Eliot had no concern

with the extension of the science to which he has given such light. His purpose was utterly practical, to preach to the Indians. They must not only understand; they must be convinced. The subject was religion. Vast new ideas and concepts must be made clear. The emotions must be touched. Will power must be awakened. Where were the words and how could he find them without written texts? Cockenoe, his boy teacher, was a stranger to Christianity, and the entire vocabulary of presentation and explanation of spiritual truth was missing. Even when by patient inquiry he found the words, where were the analogies in Indian experience through which the meaning could be clarified?

Translation would present this difficulty immediately. One of his first exercises in translation was the Lord's Prayer. The first phrase, "Our Father, who art in heaven," can be expressed in another tongue, literally, perhaps without loss of meaning, although the father relationship applied to deity would be entirely strange to Indian comprehension. "Thy kingdom come," is an enigma. "What is the kingdom of heaven?" a puzzled Indian once asked Eliot in the question period following a sermon. The remainder of the prayer is full of enigmas for a congregation of Indians. "Why must we forgive our enemies?" another asked. Indians feel no such desire.

The translation of Genesis I:1, word for word as it is written, "In the beginning God created the heaven and the earth," might be accomplished with literal clarity. One of the Indian gods was a creator. But what of the "The Lord is my shepherd, I shall not want"? The care of sheep and the whole panorama of shepherd life has no relation with Indian experience, and such a relationship between God and man has no parallel in Indian thought of God. Words have precise meanings; they also have atmospheres, and their atmosphere for one race may be totally different for another. With a multitude of words at his command, their literal meanings known, the preacher or translator would still be helpless without an intimate knowledge of the life and culture of the people to whom he would explain abstract concepts. Ideally, he must know their language almost as well as his own. Robert Frost once said, and wisely, "Poetry is what disappears in translation," and of what material could this be more true than of the Bible, which is so often poetry, even in its prose. The parables of Jesus clarified spiritual truth to those who listened on the mount. New analogies would be needed for John Eliot's congregation at Waban's wigwam.

That he could meet this requirement sometimes brilliantly can be seen in the sketchy reports his friends wrote of an occasional sermon in such a situation. At the end of his first recorded sermon at Waban's wigwam, a question arose that would be asked him scores of times. How do we believe what eyes cannot see? When you see a big wigwam, John Eliot answered, do you think the raccoons built it, or the foxes, or that it built itself? Certainly not. Look at the house of this great world. Look at the sun, the moon, the stars. Doesn't it look as though a very powerful, wise Being built it? We can't see Him with our eyes, but look at his work.[6]

One of John Eliot's gifts for what he was trying to do was his concreteness in clarifying new and strange ideas in terms close to what he knew of the Indians' forest lives. It is a great pity that we have not even a single full example of these forest sermons — only a few hastily written jottings, set down by those who did not know the language and could only observe the effect on the hearers. Fortunately, John Eliot supplied most illuminating lists of the questions the Indians asked him. No doubt he was helped by them, as we are, for every question is a searchlight into some dark corner of an Indian's mind.

Slowly the challenge of the language yielded to patient un-

tiring study and painful first exercises in translation.  Before
his first sermon was preached to an Indian congregation, he
had prepared translations of portions of the catechism, short
passages of Scripture and the Lord's Prayer.  In the extant accounts of his first sermons there is no mention of singing, but
very probably he was ready with a metrical translation of a
few verses from a psalm, an exercise that would have greatly
pleased the Indians.  The Lord's Prayer, translated probably
with Cockenoe's help, suggests what had preceded the victory
it memorializes.  Before he could translate this short piece he
had made enough discoveries to fill many pages of the grammar he would not dare to attempt until twenty years later.

Here is the Lord's Prayer, as it appears in John Eliot's
translation of the Bible, Cambridge, 1663.  The English
translation is from the German of Johann Christoph Adelung
of Dresden, Berlin, 1812.[7]

Matthew 6:9–13

Our father   heaven in   hallowed
*Nushun*      *kesukqut;*   *Quttianatamunach*

thy name      come           thy kingdom
*koowesuonk;*  *Peyaumootch*  *kukketossutamoonk;*

thy will                done earth on
*Kuttenantamoonk*    *nen nach ohkeit*

as        heaven in    our food
*neane*   *kesukqut;*   *Nummeetsuongash*

daily           give    us    this this   day
*asekesukokish*  *asamaiinean*  *yeuyeu*   *kesukod;*

and    forgive           us      our
*Kah*  *ahquontamaiiunnean*   *nummatch*

sins          as        wicked-doers
*eseongash*   *neane*   *matchenekuk queagigu*

| we forgive | | them | also | lead |
|---|---|---|---|---|
| *nutahquontamounnonog;* | | | *Ahque* | *sagkom-* |

| | us | not | temptation in |
|---|---|---|---|
| *pagunaiinnean* | | *en* | *qutchhuaonganit;* |

| Oh | deliver | us | evil |
|---|---|---|---|
| *Wehe* | *pohquohwussinnean* | *wutch match* | |

| from | for | thine | kingdom |
|---|---|---|---|
| *itut;* | *New wutche* | *kutahtaun* | *ketassootamoonk* |

| and | power | and | glory |
|---|---|---|---|
| *kah* | *menukesuonk* | *kah* | *sohsumoonk* |

| forever | Amen |
|---|---|
| *nicheme.* | *Amen.* |

He had made such preparation as he could, alone in his study or with his teacher. Ease and some degree of mastery would come only as he faced a company of Indians and realized that they understood him. It was time to put himself to the public test. Years after when he came to the last page of *The Indian Grammar Begun* he wrote these words, no doubt experienced for himself before he wrote them as counsel to others: "We must not sit still, and look for miracles; Up and be doing, and the Lord will be with thee. Prayer and Pains, through Faith in Christ Jesus, will do anything." [8] In this spirit he went forth, when the day came.

## AT WABAN'S WIGWAM

J OHN ELIOT's first formal share in "hopeful beginnings," as
John Winthrop called his first sermons in the Algonquian
tongue, took place at the wigwam of petty chieftain Waban at
Nonantum (now Newton) on October 28, 1646. He had
tried out his ability to preach in the native tongue at Dorchester Mill a month earlier, but his effort had been without
success. The Indians "regarded it not," he said, "gave no
heed unto it, but were weary and despised what I said." This
failure made the October 28th occasion a stern test. Prepara-
tions had been more carefully made, especially in announcement to the neighboring Indians.

This was sixteen years after the founding of the Massachusetts Bay colony and fifteen years after John Eliot's arrival in
Boston. For him it was the beginning of more than forty
years of missionary endeavor. He was not being sent by either
colony or church leaders. No one had appointed him to this
task. He was a private citizen, making an individual response
under pressure of his own conscience and his personal sense of
one man's responsibility under the charter obligation.

Fortunately, an account of this day's sermon is extant, written by Thomas Shepard, minister at Cambridge, who was
present. "Four of us," he wrote, "having sought God, went
unto the Indians inhabiting our bounds with desire to make
known the things of their peace to them." The two others
besides John Eliot and Shepard were Daniel Gookin, years
later to be appointed by the General Court to have general

supervision of the Indian towns and to hold courts within them, and either John Wilson, pastor of the Boston church, or Elder Heath of Roxbury. The four men had come on horseback the distance of five miles from Boston to Nonantum, located near Watertown mill on the south side of the Charles River. When they were within a short distance of the high stockade enclosing the wigwams, five or six of the chief men of the village advanced to meet them, using English salutations and leading them to the wigwam of Waban, their minister of justice. This wigwam, larger than the others, was central and stood a little apart from the others. Behind it on both sides dark trees stretched to the horizon. Directly in front a small company of Indian men, women and children sat on the ground, their blankets drawn around them. A few men leaned against trees farther away, almost out of hearing. It was a solemn moment, made more so by the silence of the wilderness.

John Eliot stepped forward, greeted them as friends, lifted his arms and began the service with a prayer in English, not yet daring, as he said later, to express his heart before God in the Algonquian tongue. After the prayer came the reading of the Ten Commandments, with a brief explanation of each. John Eliot was, of course, well aware that the entire Decalogue at one reading could take scant hold on either the understanding or imagination of these men and women before him, but he was not one to deal piecemeal with fundamental Christian ethics or with what he called the plan of Salvation. Face them with the whole of it at first and then proceed with details one by one later. That was always his way.

For the Indian children squatting on the front row immediately before him, he began with the first three questions of the catechism.

"Who made you and all the world? God.

"Who doe you look should save you and redeeme you from sinne and hell? Jesus Christ.

"How many commandments hath God given you to keepe? Ten." [1]

Question and answer were recited by the preacher several times and then the question was addressed to the children who tried to answer in chorus, as he directed them to do. This was all in their own tongue.

The sermon had for its text, Ezekiel 37:9, the story of Ezekiel's vision of the dry bones. As the preacher read the passage from the Bible, beginning, "Then said he unto me, prophesy unto the wind," he saw each of the company turn to another, then look at Waban, who smiled in return. Only later John Eliot learned that the word *wind* in Algonquian is *Waban,* which, enigmatical as it must have been in that connection to the congregation, gave something of a local touch to Ezekiel's vision. The dry bones story apparently pleased the Indians, whatever they may have made of it. It also gave them a new name, Ezekiel, with which to endow the next born Indian child or some adult in the congregation. Very soon every group to which John Eliot preached would be full of Old Testament characters.

The story told and commented on briefly, the preacher abandoned Ezekiel and his vision and for an hour and a quarter introduced his hearers to the God of the white man, maker of all men and of the world, a being of almighty power, terrible in his wrath toward them that disobey him; to Jesus Christ, the only means of recovery from sin and death and eternal punishment; and to the joys of heaven for the redeemed and the tortures of hell for those who are not saved. Whatever the text, this was always the sermon, a God of power, man a lost soul, Christ the only savior, heaven or hell, according to man's own choice.

Perhaps it is impossible even to try to imagine how such a preachment would sound to these children of darkness who were hearing it for the first time. No matter how gently it was spoken, it was a frightening doctrine. The religion of the Indians is not theological, not in the least. They believed in unseen power truly enough — power of devils, of witches, good spirits, evil spirits; this power invested places and objects, and there was peril in it. By performing ceremonial acts, man could free himself from its dangers; hence (in part) the observance of taboo in every aspect of their lives. Christianity belonged to another world entirely. Indians had supreme gods, both for good and evil, but these deities did not punish men for wrongdoing. The family and the tribe took care of that. Indian religion assumed no ethical control, demanded no obedience to any counterpart of the Ten Commandments. A god who must be obeyed, whose laws were known, and who would administer eternal punishment for failure to keep them was stranger than Western thought can well conceive.

There is no indication that John Eliot or any other early missionary preacher began his preparation for his mission by any attempt to learn wherein Indian religion consisted; what it taught; what assumptions about God and man, present and future, life and death, the individual Indian possessed from the total culture of his race. Roger Williams made a few notations as to Indian religion in his *Key to the Indian Language,* enough to show that he had given thought to the subject, but in this book he was concerned with other matters primarily. Doubtless other first-generation men had also given thought to what we now call anthropology, but rarely. The current view was that Indians were heathen. Their beliefs were of the devil, who very probably, said Cotton Mather, planted them on this continent. Away with such false ideas. Christianity is the only true religion.

After sixteen years' living as neighbor to the white man,

the average New England Indian knew that the white man's god lived in heaven, and that someone else called Jesus was a god also. White men prayed. They did not work on Sunday. What the General Court called *blasphemy* could send an Indian to the gallows. Why? How could he know? All this was very vague in his mind and his thought went no further. What John Eliot, a gentle, friendly man, was telling his company at Waban's wigwam on this day was frightening. He spoke terrible things and they listened in consternation.

"Have you understood?" he asked, as he stopped short after an hour and a quarter. In a chorus of voices they answered, "Yes." He had at least pronounced well enough for them to recognize the words. "Have you any questions?"

Immediately questions came, and the first one, naturally enough, "How may we come to know Jesus Christ?" He gave them two ways. "First, by reading the Bible, which is God's book. Of course you cannot do that yet, but until you learn how to read, think about what I have told you. Think in the morning, when you wake up; think when you go into the fields; think when you lie down on your mats again at night. Second, pray."

An Indian interrupted. "Does the white man's god hear Indian prayers?" he said. This was just the question John Eliot wanted.

"Certainly," he answered. "Look at this basket. You made it. White straws, black straws. You know where they came from, and how you put them together. Someone who didn't make it, wouldn't know. He wouldn't understand how you could do it. God made Indians. He knows all about them. Of course he knows your language and understands every word."

More questions followed, and there would have been still more, but after three hours, it was better to leave them with an appetite, and the meeting was concluded with another prayer.

Before the assembly broke up, John Eliot produced apples and sweetmeats for the children, tobacco for the men and other small surprises he had brought with him. He also accepted the invitation to come again and named the day a fortnight hence when he would return.

"So we departed with many welcomes," Thomas Shepard wrote. Just as they were leaving, Waban approached and said, "We need more ground to build our town on."

"I will speak to the General Court about that," [2] John Eliot answered and they were off.

A simple beginning it had been, and moderately hopeful it seemed to the four men, as they rode away into the woods in the October twilight. Looked back upon, as John Eliot would do many times, these three hours had opened new doors for him and forecast a stern program of unremitting labor for the whole of the second half of his life. These men and women must have the Bible in their hands, in their own tongue and they must be taught to read it. So far as we know, translating it was not yet even a dim purpose in his own thought. Even several years later, after he had begun the translation, he thought finishing it was impossible for him. Yet he began. "More ground to build a town on," and his answer, "I will speak to the General Court about it." That answer opened another door. He would walk through that one too, and before the task beyond had ended, there would be fourteen Indian towns. October 28, 1646, had been a beginning beyond what he could have imagined or dared to think.

Something had been planted in this first meeting, and John Eliot was wise enough not to let it wither and be lost. Two weeks later, he came again with his three companions. A much larger crowd of Indians had assembled and sat waiting. Four seats had been placed in the front for the white men. They had stood the first time. After the opening prayer, John Eliot heard the children recite their answers to the first three questions of the catechism given them two weeks before: Who made you and all the world? Who doe you look should save you and redeeme you from sinne and hell? How many commandments hath God given you to keepe? Each child answered individually, and then all of them together in shrill chorus. The parents and newcomers present listened also, and learned. When this was finished, the preacher read and explained another question for the following week. Each child received an apple or a sweetmeat as on the former occasion.

The second sermon was announced as good news. How may evil men come to be good, be happy while they live and go to heaven when they die? He made it all as simple as though to children. Keep the Ten Commandments, repent of your sins, pray to God and believe in Jesus Christ. Many of the Indians seemed moved by his words. They wept freely as he spoke of God's love as well as his wrath. The first question came from an old man.

"I am near death. Is it too late for me to seek Christ?" This question came often and John Eliot was always ready for it with a comforting answer. As in all such question periods there were puzzled inquiries as to why, if we are all children of one father, white men know about the Ten Commandments and Indians do not. Why are white men sometimes bad? Childish questions perhaps, but a chance for something beyond the mere answer, if the preacher is wise, and John Eliot knew how to make these questions lead to something that might lighten their darkness beyond the literal answer. Always too, there were questions about nature's wonders. Where does the thunder come from? How comes it to pass that sea water is salt and land water fresh? Why are strawberries sweet and cranberries sour? If the water is higher than the earth, why does it not overflow all the earth?

John Eliot's answer to this last question was made graphic by the use of an apple and a somewhat pre-Copernican explanation of the sun moving around the globe of the earth. He also satisfied his hearers as to the possible flooding of the earth by saying that God in his mighty power had "digged a hole for all sea waters and had made it so deep that the water could not get out to overflow the whole earth." The answer to the terrifying noise of thunder, the salt of the sea, the sweetness of strawberries and sourness of cranberries, and many other natural marvels was "no reason but the wonderfull worke of God that made them so."

This answer probably satisfied John Eliot as well as his dark questioners, for he was no scientist and to magnify the wonderful power of God was enough. The mysteries of nature troubled the Indians and the fact that they brought their uneasiness to their teacher this early in their acquaintance suggests that he had at least begun to put them at ease with him. He answered their queries with unwearied patience, never forgetting that his purpose was religious enlightenment. "What do you remember of what I told you a week ago?" he asked. Before answering they talked among themselves and then said, "Wonderful things," and thanked him for coming. "Do you believe what I told you?" he persisted, and the answer was, "Yes," whatever assent may have meant at that early stage.

The afternoon now being far spent, he closed the service with another reminder of the terror of God's wrath, his mercy to the penitent, the tortures of hell and the bliss of heaven. A prayer fifteen minutes long was always his way of ending the service. On this as on other preaching occasions there was much weeping, always noted with surprise by the scribe. Indian tears came easily at the picturing of sinful man, his heart stony in spite of the punishment awaiting him unless he repented. One thinks of the classic remark of Wequash, Roger Williams' Indian friend, burdened with his own sense of guilt and helpless under it, "Me so big naughty heart, me heart all one stone," he had said, hopelessly.

John Eliot met self-confessed stony hearts every preaching day, and the confession always came with flooding tears, but he did not soften the severity of God's wrath to comfort the weeper. Only the repentance of the sinner could do that. Human wickedness, God's anger because of it, eternal punishment ahead unless sinners repented, these "truths" were never absent from his sermons which were also reported as delivered with "much affection." Concreteness in the presentation of eternal torture, of course, frightened the Indians who accepted what they heard as literally as it was spoken. Righteousness was also presented literally. Behavior was the test. Did they keep the Ten Commandments? This was the supreme test. If not, God was angry. Did they pray? The emphasis on prayer as the mark of a Christian's way of life was always fundamental; hence the caption "Praying Indians," by which they came to be known. Did they keep the Sabbath? For Indians the easiest test of all. "We never work on any day if we can help it," an Indian is reported to have answered once when this question was asked, "so that we can easily agree not to work on that day." Did they believe in Jesus Christ? Over and over these questions were asked, as they had been at these first two meetings at Waban's wigwam.

More important than anything he had told them was the friendliness his coming had meant to these people. They sensed his respect for their attention, his confidence in their willingness to listen. There was not a hint of condescension in his manner, not a word of apology for what his white brethren had done amiss in their dealings with Indians. Always straightforward, he spoke what he believed and his plain honesty was rewarded by their willingness to ask more. Perhaps the hardest question ever put to him was asked more than once, "Why has no white man ever told us this before? Many years ago white men came. Why did you wait to tell us?" There being no answer, John Eliot said simply. "I am sorry."

From the brief report of the scribe for each of these meetings, it is clear that John Eliot was preaching sermons quite out of line with what the colonial clergy usually preached to their congregations, and what he himself probably preached in Roxbury. These sermons to the Indians at Waban's wigwam are distinctly evangelistic. Repent and be saved. Turn and be converted. Escape hell and get to heaven. Not one word about the Calvinistic Five Points. In the village meetinghouses on Sunday, the whole town listened to an exposition of Calvinistic doctrine aimed primarily at the covenanted group of members inside the circle. This was Calvinism as yet unmodified to give man a chance to choose salvation for himself. (It would be a full century before the biblical "whosoever will" invitation to the sinner would have the accent, and men and women be pled with to escape eternal damnation by accepting it.) Terror of hell and hope of heaven would bring scores (at least while the eighteenth-century revivals of George Whitefield lasted) into the church fellowship.

In these seventeenth-century sermons to Indians John Eliot was reducing the Calvinistic system to something far simpler and doing it a full century earlier. Not that he was an innovator in doctrine or a revolutionist. Far from it. He was a practical teacher, facing a huddled group of blanketed Indians whom he hoped to help toward a better life. Clearly the

Calvinistic Five Points would be less than a guide they could understand, let alone relate to their own lives in the wigwam. One can recognize Calvinism in the simple substitute he offered. *Total depravity* becomes all men are sinful before God, but repentance opens the way to forgiveness. *Limited atonement* becomes atonement without limits. Anyone who repents and has faith is on the way to salvation. Not a word about *predestination, irresistibility of grace, perseverance of the saints.* One long look into the Indian faces before him would be sufficient reason for silence on these imponderables. Even so apparently simple a word as *faith* could be a stumbling block. "Do I have faith?" an Indian once asked, and his query opens a door into vast empty spaces. One would like to know John Eliot's response to this elemental question from another world of thought and experience, but it is not recorded.

We have no Roxbury sermons of John Eliot to his own people, but there is scant likelihood that he preached to his congregation on Meeting House Hill as he was doing at Waban's wigwam. He always insisted that a sermon should be "well-studied," and scholar that he was in sound doctrine, doubtless his sermons there showed such study, attention to logic and precision of application to the daily lives of his fellow townsmen. There would have been no success with the Indians had he preached of doctrine familiar to his Roxbury people since they were children in the pew. Simplicity, urgency, literalness were prime requisites, and apparently comprehension had been sufficient here at the wigwam to bring tears and the equivalent of the biblical question, "What must I do to be saved?"

As the four men talked together on their ride home after this second preaching, they decided to continue their visits through the winter, "frosts and snows" notwithstanding, lest the "fire go out of the Indians' hearts for want of a little fuel."

The next day one of the Indians walked to John Eliot's home in Roxbury in great troublement for his sins. Weeping exceedingly, he reported that all night the Indians had not slept, partly with trouble of mind, and partly with wondering at the things they had heard preached that day. The next day another Indian came to report that the wicked Indians had already begun to oppose the preaching, especially the pow-wows and medicine men who feared to lose their authority. It would ever be so and increasingly. Some among the local English settlers would also oppose them, not for the work's sake, but because of what possibly might come of Indian opposition. The local Indians in Massachusetts had been friendly to the whites for the most part, but there had been occasional incidents that aroused apprehensions. John Eliot was too wise and too practical to foresee an early success, but he was encouraged by these "heart breakings" among the Indians for their sins, and opposition from any source was but a further challenge.

On his third meeting, November 26, he found more wigwams built and more Indians waiting to hear him. He took for his theme the temptations of the devil, and since Indian thought of unseen power included a good god and an evil god, this sermon came closer to their understanding than the two previously preached. His words brought as first questions, What is a spirit? Should we believe dreams? May we pray to the devil? He probably answered these questions as a Calvinist, supporting his answers with Bible texts. The scribe did not report the answers. How do you English know so much about God and we so little? Most urgently they repeated their desire to have a town of their own. We want to learn to spin, said the women, and at once both sides felt the solid ground beneath their feet more firmly.

Very soon after this third meeting more Indian representatives came to Roxbury to talk with John Eliot. One named Wampas wished to offer up his children, aged nine, eight, five and four to be educated. If they stayed in the wigwam, he said, they would grow up rude and wicked; he wished them to learn better by living with the English. Two young Indians who accompanied Wampas volunteered to serve the English in their homes and thereby learn the English religion. Two elders of the church granted their request, took them into their homes, and Wampas was promised education for his children as soon as arrangements could be made. He was satisfied. Thus the door opened wider.

Meanwhile, Waban, keeper of peace in the village, together with other Indian leaders of the neighborhood, on their own initiative, had drawn up a code of ten laws for their better governance. Undoubtedly the Ten Commandments had determined the number. These were not religious laws, but a code of behavior enforcing cleanliness, neatness and decency in dress and behavior, industry. Each departure from the code demanded payment of a fine, usually five shillings. These five examples suggest the area of reform.

1. If any man be idle a weeke, at most a fortnight, hee shall pay five shillings.

3. For wife beating, including only one serious offence, the offender shall have his hands tied behind him, and be carried to the place of justice to be severely punished.

4. Every young man, if not another's servant, and if unmarried, hee shall be compelled to set up a *wigwam* and plant for himself, and not live shifting up and down to other wigwams.

5. If any woman shall not have her hair tied up but hang loose or be cut as men's hair, she shall pay five shillings.

7. All those men that weare long locks shall pay five shillings.[3]

Some, possibly all ten of these rules, had their source in the
observance of English manners and customs, and were a ges-
ture toward civilization, apparently sparked by the coming of
the English visitors. The English residents who had insisted
so strongly that civilization should precede any religious
teaching, might have been silenced or at least encouraged by
this step, Indian inspired as it seemed to be. More encouraging to John Eliot was the report of Indian prayers from two
young Englishmen who had spent the night in Waban's wigwam after the last preaching meeting. They had written
down these prayers to show him.

> *Amanaomen Jehovah tahassen metogh.*
> Take away, Lord, my stony heart.
>
> *Chechesom Jehovah kekeowhogkow*
> Wash, Lord, my soule.[4]

John Eliot had avoided giving first listeners a model for personal prayer, lest they learn and use it by rote. Clearly these
two petitions had their source in the sermons he had preached
to them.

At the fourth meeting held December 9, the Indians
offered all their children to be educated by the English, saying they were able to pay nothing in return. The response of
the English was immediate; a school was already in the
planning stage. Less than six weeks had passed since the first
preaching service, but the word had already gone far. Some
Indians from other neighborhoods had come by, remained a
few days and watched Waban's Indians on the Sabbath day.
How did they keep it? Why were they cutting their hair?
Some came to revile, chiefly the powwows or sorcerers, who
would lose both gain and prestige by this shift to Christian

ways. Others came of curiosity. Clearly there would be trouble ahead, but a beginning had been made. Shortly afterward John Eliot began to preach also regularly at Neponset, a small village on the Neponset River separating Dorchester from Milton.

At the close of his account of this fourth meeting, the scribe, possibly still Thomas Shepard, invited English readers to help in the work so encouragingly begun. We shall need money to educate the Indian children already given to us, he wrote. This will mean clothing as well as teachers. Undoubtedly other Indians will soon ask for the same chance and send us more children. Until a project is fully organized, contributions may be sent to the President of Harvard College, who will make it available to us. The request was timidly made. It would be met more generously than anyone had dared to imagine.

Meanwhile through snow and ice and winter cold, John Eliot continued in alternate weeks to mount his horse and thread the rugged trail through the woods to Waban's cabin where more and more Indians waited. His entry in the church book shows his spirit (page 246): "We never had a bad day to go preach to the Indians all the winter. Praised be the Lord."

## THE SOCIETY FOR THE
## PROPAGATION OF THE GOSPEL

NEWS OF the favorable response to the sermons preached in the Algonquian tongue spread quickly. John Eliot and his companions, of course, reported them to their own congregations, to brother ministers and magistrates on their return. Those who had previously known that John Eliot was learning the Indian language for the purpose of preaching, even those who were skeptical of his ability to be persuasive in it, and also those (and there were many) who doubted whether Indians could be reached by any means whatsoever, all were waiting with some degree of interest for report of these first efforts at Waban's wigwam. The announced success surprised everyone. It also gave comfortable satisfaction to those who still smarted under the criticism for the long delay in beginning the work of evangelization. At last the world might know that New England had not forgotten her errand into the wilderness.

At the synod held in Cambridge in May, 1647, six months after this beginning, a number of Waban's Indians, men, women and children were taken to one of the sessions as a congregation. John Eliot preached to them in Algonquian, catechized the children and held the usual question period after the sermon. This public exhibition impressed clergy and lay representatives who were present, as it was intended to do. The serious demeanor of the Indians, the ready responses of the half-naked Indian children, the strange music of the psalm sung in Algonquian and perhaps also the fluency of John Eliot in a language of which they could distinguish only the untranslated words, God, Christ Jesus, Jehovah — all this would be reported back through ministers and laymen to the meetinghouse congregations of the entire colony.[1]

To tell the mother country was also important, indeed urgent. *New England's First Fruits,* printed in 1643, had made large promises toward Indian conversion, but what were the details behind it? The lot fell to Edward Winslow of the 1620 Pilgrim company to carry the news of John Eliot's success back to England almost at once and in person. As the next few months proved, he was the best of messengers for the purpose. Deeply religious, but without a hint of religiosity, he was an eminently practical man, a diplomat, a gentleman of pleasant approach and wide resourcefulness.

In December, 1646, he had been newly appointed agent of the colony to succeed Thomas Weld and Hugh Peter, his immediate predecessors, who had made serious mistakes and accomplished little toward a response to an appeal for financial help for the colonies.[2] Some monies had been collected in a project to send over "poor children," but for unexplained reasons, the poor children had not arrived and somehow the money collected had miscarried. Bad feeling had been aroused in England, and the new agent's first duty would be to change it.

Fortunately for his success, on the eve of Edward Winslow's sailing, he secured the hastily written manuscript telling of the first four meetings at Waban's wigwam. On shipboard he put them in shape for printing and immediately on his arrival in London had them published. Wisely he saw to it that an introductory epistle was added, addressed to the Lords and Commons, then meeting in the Long Parliament. The tract was entitled *The Day-Breaking, if not the Sun Rising of the Gospell with the Indians in New-England.*[3] This title attracted attention at once, in spite of the large number of pamphlets which were pouring forth in a flood from London presses at this date.

The English, understandably enough, were less realistic about Indians than New Englanders, and the tale of penitent tears running down Indian cheeks, their children being catechized, Indian arms raised in prayer to the white man's god, Indians keeping the Sabbath — all this matched the English hope, long deferred, of a great harvest of heathen souls. Wisely Edward Winslow did not let the tract carry the news alone. Before it was off the press and for sale at bookstalls, he had begun to pass the word along personally to his wide circle of acquaintances, many of whom were members of Parliament.

Three months later he received the manuscript of a second report of Indian conversions which he also printed immediately. This one was entitled, *The Clear Sun-Shine of the Gospel Breaking forth upon the Indians in New-England.*[4] This time there were two dedicatory epistles, one to the "Right Honourable Lords and Commons" and one "To the godly and well affected of this Kingdom of England," both signed by twelve English ministers, Church of England and Presbyterian. A long letter of John Eliot's was also included, giving many details and serving as a first person authentication to his statement, "The finger of God is here." The postscript by Thomas Shepard also corroborated the story. Both men made it lively and hopeful.

> The Indians have utterly forsaken their powwows.
> They catechize their own children.
> They have set up morning and evening prayers in their wigwams.
> They not only keep the Sabbath themselves, but have made a law to punish those who do not. Whoever profanes it must pay twenty shillings.

They begin to grow industrious and are making articles to
sell all the year long. In winter, brooms, stoves, eelpots,
baskets; in the spring they sell cranberries, fish, strawberries.
The women are learning to spin.

Sample questions from the Indians after a preaching meeting
may well have been more interesting and illuminating than
any other details.

What was the first sin of the devil?
Why didn't God kill the devil that made all men bad, God
having all power?
Whether the devil or man was made first?
Why didn't God give all men good hearts?
From what nation did Jesus Christ come?
How far off is the place where he was born?
Where is he now?
If a man were enclosed in iron a foot thick and thrown into
the fire, what would become of his soul? Could it get out or
not?
Whither do little children goe when they dye, seeing they
have not sinned?
What do English men think of Mr. Eliot who comes among
wicked Indians to teach them?

Something very different from Indians in paint and feathers,
dancing a hoop dance or shooting arrows, as well as something
about the preaching of John Eliot comes along with these
questions.

Edward Winslow's design was to get a bill through Parliament which would insure the continuance of John Eliot's
work. Without immediate financial aid he was already helpless, and New England could not be counted on to furnish
more than the merest fragment of the sums needed for cloth-

ing, tools, spinning wheels, hoes, mattocks, shovels, salaries of teachers, wages for Indian laborers. Everything was needed and at once, before the first interest of the Indians faded.

The question of English financial help for this work was first raised in Parliament in March, 1647/8, and referred to the Committee for Foreign Plantations. Edward Winslow himself had helped to draft the bill which was ready for its first reading in August. Again and again a date was set for reading it, but postponement came until December, when it was thrown out as not giving enough power to the feoffees. A second bill, drafted in April, 1649, made speedier progress, probably because of the spur offered by the printing, again by Edward Winslow, of a third pamphlet entitled, *The Glorious Progress of the Gospel amongst the Indians in New England*.[5] Edward Winslow's name on the title page, three letters by John Eliot and one from Thomas Mayhew, Jr., missionary on Martha's Vineyard, made up the text, together with an appendix signed G.D.

John Eliot supplied many more questions, "to give a taste of their knowledge," he said, adding that he has "slipped many and very materiall ones." We wish he had not, for these questions give more than a "taste of their knowledge." One would like to compare them with a list of similarly puzzled questions asked a modern missionary by members of a race hearing of Christianity for the first time. No one of the following Indian questions selected from *The Eliot Tracts*, would be very likely to appear in the list.

What is Salvation?
How shall I bring my Heart to love Prayer?
You say our Body is made of Clay; what is the Sunne or
    Moone made of?
How long was Adam good before he sinned?
Doth the Devill dwell in us as we dwell in a House?

When the Soule goes to Heaven, what does it say when it
  comes there?

And what doth a wicked Soule say when it cometh into Hell?

Why must we love our enemies, and how shall we do it?

May a good man sin sometimes?

Shall we see God in Heaven?

I find I want wisdome, what shall I do to be wise?

Why is God so angry with murtherers?

Doe not Englishmen spoile their soules, to say a thing cost
  more than it did? and is it not all one as to steale?

How shall the Resurrection be, and when?

What is Law?

Why doth God punish in Hell for ever?  Man doth not so, but
  after a time lets them out of prison again?  Why will not
  God let them out again?

Doth the Soule in Heaven know things done here on Earth?

What if a Minister wear long hayre, as some other men do,
  what will God say?

In his "Dedicatory letter to the Right Honourable the Parliament of England and the Council of State," Edward
Winslow added what would have been a new argument to
many for continuing the work among the Indians; namely,
their possible descent from one of the ten tribes of Israel.
Thomas Thorowgood's book,[6] giving his evidence for this
theory was not yet published, but Edward Winslow's knowledge of it and his decision to use it for the few who might be
interested suggests his alert resourcefulness. A few readers of
the academic sort might be won by this hint.

The second bill was finally read on July 27, 1649, and ordered printed.  It was entitled "An Act for the promoting and
propagating the Gospel of Jesus Christ in New England."
This act provided for a corporation of sixteen persons, including a governor, treasurer and fourteen assistants with

Church of St. John the Baptist, Widford, Hertfordshire,
England, where John Eliot was baptized in 1604
*Courtesy of Robert Daintree, Widford*

Church at Nazeing, Essex, England, John Eliot's childhood home
*Courtesy of the Essex County Council and of Mr. H. F. Hallyar*

Gateway, Jesus College, Cambridge University
*Courtesy of the Proprietors of* Country Life, *London*

Mr: John Eliot he came to N.E. in the 9th month, 1631. he left his intended wife in England, to come the next yeare; he adjoyned to the Church at Boston & though willing in soe ma... of mr wilson the Pastor of yt church who was gone back to England for his wife & family. yet most humble mr wilson returned, & by yt time this church at Boston was intend:d to call him to office; his frinds yt came over & setled at Rockxbrough, whereas he was pre engaged & if he were not called to office before they came, he was to joyne with them: whereupon the church at Rockxbrough called him to be Teacher & the 2d of the 9th same after he was ordained to yt office in the church. Also his wife came along & the rest of his frinds the same time, & soe after their coming they were married in the 8th month, 1632. Hanah his first borne daughter was borne the 17 day of the 7th month ano. 1633. John his first borne son was borne the 31 day of the 8th month ano 1636. Joseph his 2d son was borne in the 20th day of the 10th month, ano. 1638. Samuel his 3d son, was borne the 22 day of the 4th month ano: 1641. Aaron his 4th sonne was borne the 19 of the 12. ano 1643. Benjamin his 5th sonne was borne the 29 of the 11th 1646.




Mris Ann Eliot, the wife of mr John Eliot




Mr George Alcock he came in the first company ano. 1630. he left his wife big in England. his wife dyed some after he came to this land; under the people of Rock-brough joyned to the church at Dorchester untill there we God first gave them opertunity to be a church amoung them selves; he was by that church chosen to be a Deacon & soe to regard the bretheren at Rockxbrough. And after he adjoyned himselfe to the church at Rockxbrough, he was ordained a Deakon of this church: he made two voyages to England, upon just calling therunto, therein he had much expering of Gods pservation & blessing: he brought over to this land John Alcock; he also brought over a wife by whom he had his 2d son Samuel borne in the yeare

he lived in a good & godly life & dyed in the end of the 10th month ano. 1640. & left a good savor behind him; the poore of the church much bewailing his loss




Valentine Prentise. he came to this land in the yeare, 1631. & joyned to the church in the yeare 1632. he had a sonne but one that to the s:d Pastor John & he lived most at sea. he lived a godly life & went through much affliction by bodyly infirmity, & dyed leaving a good hope of godlynes about him.

Seal of the colony of Massachusetts Bay
*Courtesy of Richard W. Hale, Jr.,*
*Archivist of the Commonwealth*

Opposite:
A page in John Eliot's hand from the records of the Eliot church in
Roxbury. *Courtesy of the Reverend John M. Coffee, Jr., Pastor*

## Christiane OOnowae Sampoowaonk.

## A Christian Covenanting Confession.

METahhawae Nunamptam kah mutœnœae nuſ=
ſonpœwam. Rom. 10. 10.

1. Paſuk nont Goo. Deut. 6:4. Jer. 10. 10.
Qut nhuœœ, Wutœſhinœœ , Wunnauhmoniin , wah
Wunneetupanatamwe Naſhauant. Matt. 28 19. 1 John
5. 7.

2. Wuſke kutchiſik, ayum Goo Keſuk kah
Ohke ahche wunnegen. Gen. 1. 1. 31.

3. Nanawunnuwaheau Adam yeu agueyeue
muttaohke. Gen. 1. 26. 28

4. Adam pannuppe ſamrweuſh , qut teanuk
matcheſu kah awakompanau. Gen 3. Ecleſ 7. 29.

5. Adam nœœmaſik wunukuœwa uammatche=
ſeonk , kah wutonkapnnaonk. Rom. 5. 2

6. Neuaj neetimun ut mat theſeonganit. Pſal.
51 5.

7. Neeſe chippiſſa numuœ theſeonk.
⎰ 1. Wutchaubukkue matcheſeonk. Rom. 3. 10
⎱ 2. Uſſuwae matcheſeonk. Matt. 15. 19.

8. Yeuſh naū pe nuttumhouamun nicheme
awakomppanaonk chepiohkeomukqut. Rom. 6. 23

9. Nunamptam wame woh nutomohkemun
wuſſittumwae keſukkodtut. 1 Cor. 15.

1. IEſus Chriſt Wunnaumonuh Goo. Pſal 2. 6, 7.
Qut wuiketompaoœ, newaj manit kah woſ
ketomp paluœœ Heb. 2. 16, 17.

2. Wuranôſuongaſh Jeſus Chriſt oiſhwinaſh,
Sephauſuwaenuſh, Heb. 7. 1, 2, 2. Quoſhodtumwaenuœ
Acts 3. 22. Kehaikutœmônu Iſai. 33. 22.

3. Jeſus Chriſt pahke kenoiweetamwanduk=
qun , kah kuttoodtehteaunſhikqun œuppoonk nupprœ
wonsakqueœg , kah yeuſh waj kuttunhouaunſhikqun
wame nummatcheſeongaſh , ahquontamôadtio. Rev.
1. 5. Matt. 3. 15.

4. Yeuyeu naſhpe wunaonchemœkae wuſke
wunnœwaonk, Jeſus Chriſt kœweekœmukqun wame
ziuſkoiantamunit kah wannamptamáe quiſhkenut en
Godut. Acts 17. 30. Iſai. 56. 1, 2, 3, 4, 5, 6, 7, 8.

5. Yeuſh waj , neenawun yeu otanat apeuſk ,
aſſœweramun wekontamweſhnukkiſh pinomun nuk heg
kanonog en Godut , mehquontamunat Sabbath ,
pahketeaunat tohſohke pomantamog. Wonk nukkiſh=
piſſuonſttumun mœ̂nat Sa. S.bbath daykiſh ( ne wob
g nag ) uſſenat wame Sabbath dayœ peantamœ aſſe=
ongaſh , neaunak wuttinnœwaonk Goo, aninnunuuk=
queœz wunneetutanatamwe Naſhauanit.

Ne naſhpe wunnœwaonk , nummegamun nuhhog
kanonœg kah nunneechanog en Jeſus Chriſt, mo=
œuweekœorgene pomoꝩonat teſohke pomantamog.

Woi Lord Jeſus Chriſt ⎰ ahquontamok.
⎱ keteamontaenetae.
⎱ monanitteae.

Neemunaiineau.                                    AMEN.

Matta chekewequt manunne naſſman mioſuk=
quehtoodtiꝛꝛe wame yeuſh uſſenat.

---

IBelieve with my Heart , and Confeſs with my
Mouth. Rom. 10. 10.

1. There is but one , onely , living, and
true Goo, Deut. 6. 4. Jer. 10. 10.    But He is
Father, Son, Holy Spirit. Matt. 28. 19.    1 John 5. 7.

2. In the Beginning Goo made Heaven and
Earth very Good. Gen. 1. 1, 31.

3. He made Adam to Rule this Lower world,
he being made perfectly Righteous. Gen. 1. 26. 27.

4. Adam quickly Sinned, and was puniſhed.
Gen 3. Ecleſ 7. 29.

5. Adam conveighed in to his ſin , and alſo
his guilt and puniſhment. Rom. 5. 12.

6. For this cauſe, we are all born in ſind
Tſal. 51. 5.

7. Our ſin is two fold.
⎰ 1. Original ſin. Rom 3. 10.
⎱ 2. Actual ſin. Matt. 15. 19.

8. By theſe, we deſerve Damnation in Hell
for ever. Rom. 6. 23.

9. I believe we ſhall all riſe again to Judg=
ment at the laſt day. 1 Cor. 15.

1. IEſus Chriſt is the Son of Goo. Pſal 2. 6, 7.
He become a man, and is both Goo and
Man in one Perſon. Heb. 2. 16. 17.

2. Jeſus Chriſt hath Three Offices, Prieſt
Prophet, King , Heb. 7. 1, 2, 2.    Acts 3. 22.    Iſa.
33. 22.

3. Jeſus Chriſt obeyed perfectly for us, He
payed his Death for us when He dyed for us, and
hereby He deſerved pardon for all our ſins. Rev. 1.
5. Matt. 3. 15.

4. Now by the Goſpel New Covenant Jeſus
Chriſt calleth us all to repent. and believeingly to
turn unto Goo. Acts 17. 30. Iſai. 56. 1, 2, 3, 4, 5, 6, 7.

5. For theſe cauſes, wee that dwell in this
Towne called ———— are gladly willing to bind
our ſelves to Goo, to Remember the Sabbath day
to keep it holy , ſo long as wee live.    And
alſo to bind our ſelves to each other , to meet to=
gether every Sabbath day ( when it may be done )
to doe all our Sabbath day Services , Prayers &c.
according to the word of Goo , the holy Spirit of
Goo helping us.

By this Goſpel Covenant, we do give our ſelves
and our Children to Jeſus Chriſt , to walk with
Him in Church Order, ſo long as we live.

O Lord Jeſus Chriſt , by thy Pardoning free
grace and Mercy Gracious receive us,    AMEN.

Wee compel not ſay, but meekly ſay to all
let us joyne together to doe all this.

---

**Christian Covenanting Confession**
*Courtesy of the Congregational Library, Boston*

# MAMUSSE

### WUNNEETUPANATAMWE

# UP-BIBLUM GOD

### NANEESWE

# NUKKONE TESTAMENT

### KAH WONK

# WUSKU TESTAMENT.

---

Ne quoſhkinnumuk naſhpe Wuttinneumoh *CHRIST*
noh aſooweſit

# JOHN ELIOT.

---

*CAMBRIDGE:*

Printeuoop naſhpe *Samuel Green* kah *Marmaduke John,*

1 6 6 3.

---

Title page of the Indian Bible, 1663
*Courtesy of the Boston Athenaeum Library*

## WUNNAUNCHEMOOKAONK NEAUNAK
# JOHN.

### CHAP: I.

ESKE kutchiſſik wuttinnoo-waonk ohtop, kah kuttꝏwonk ꝏweetódtamun Manit, & ne kuttꝏonk Manit ꝏꝏmꝏ.

2 *a* Yeu nan weske kutchiſſik weechayentamun God.

*b* Wame teanteaquaſſiniſh kesteauſupaſh naſhpe nagum, & matta teag kesteauineup we-be naſhpe nagum ne kesteauukup.

4 Ut wuhhogkat pomantamꝏonk ohtop, kah ne pomantamꝏonk ꝏwequáiyeumuneáop wof-ketompaog.

5 Kah wequai fohſumꝏmꝏ pohkenahtu, & pohkenai matta wutattumunumꝏun.

6 *c* Wosketomp anꝏnóp wutch Godut, uf-ſowéſu John.

7 Noh nan wutch peyau wauwaenáuneat, co-wauwónat wequái, onk woh wame wosketom-paog wunnamptamwog naſhpe nagum.

8 Matta nagum ne wequái, qut ꝏwauwó nat wequái.

9 Ne mꝏ wunnamuhkut wequái, ne wohſum-umqut niſh noh wosketomp noh páont mutta-ohkit.

10 Noh appúp muttaohket, kah *d* muttaok kesteauſip naſhpe nagum, & muttaok matta ꝏwaheuh.

11 Peyau nehenwonche wuttaiheit, & nehen-wonche wuttaiheuh matta wutattumunukꝏoh.

12 Qut neádtahſhe attumunukquit wuttin-numauoh menuhkeſuonk ꝏnaumoniiſeat God neh wanamptamunitche ꝏweſuonk.

13 Neg nékitcheg, matta naſhpe wuſqueheonk, afuh matta naſhpe weyaufue unnantamꝏonk, afuh matta naſhpe wosketompae wutten-nantamꝏonk, qut naſhpe God.

14 *e* Kah kuttꝏonk ayimꝏꝏop wey aus, kah ꝏweetomukqua (kah naumumun wuſohſtarꝏonk, fohſumꝏonk onatuh wunnukquitteghcon wutꝏſhimau) numwabéhtunk kitteamontea-nitteaonk & wunnamuhkutéyeuonk.

15 John ꝏwauwaónuh, kah mithont cowau, nꝏwau, yeuoh anꝏwaomp, noh afuhkiit mif-funkenheau onk nen, newutche na negonuh-longkup.

16 Kah wutch wunnumwameechnmuwon-ganit *f* neenawun wame nutattumunumemun kah kitteamonteanitteaonk wutch kitteamont-teanitteaonk.

17 Newutche naumatuonk aſinnum adtin

18 *g* Matta howan wunnauoh Godch noh toh ut, wun nukquttegheonin noh ſpit t ppꝏ-chinnaounit wutꝏſhimau, ꝏwalthaiuh.

19 Kah yeu ꝏwauuwaꝏnk John, Jewiog a-nꝏnahettit Sephaueuenuh & Levitioh wutch Jerufalem, natꝏtomauonat howan ken?

20 Kah fimpꝏweu kah matta kchꝏnꝏ-wóou: qut fampꝏwau, nen numwatta Chriſt.

21 Kah wunnatꝏtomauuh, toh hen funken Elias? kah nꝏwau, matta ten; fun ken noh quothódtumwaen? kah uſiinnampꝏham matta.

22 Neit nag wuttinóuh, howan ken, onk woh nunnampꝏhamauóunnonog neg anꝏ-nukqueágig? toh kuſim papaume ken?

23 *b* Nꝏwau, nen wadtauatonkquiſuonk maſhóntꝏadt ut touohkonuk, ſimpwetau-ꝏk ummay Lord, ne anꝏwop quothódtum-waen Eſayas.

24 Kah neg anꝏnitcheg Phariſefnꝏog.

25 Kah wunnatꝏtomauóuh & wuttinnóuh neit tohwutch kutcheſſummuwian, matta keu Chriſteaꝏh, qut matta Eliafuꝏ, afuh noh quoſhódtumwaénin?

26 John nah wunnampꝏhamauoh, nꝏwau, nukkutſummuwam naſhpe nippe, qut noh pa-fuk neepauit kenugke kenaru noh matta waheóg.

27 *i* Noh nan afuhkiit, miſugkeneau onk nen, noh moxinaſh kaſhpiuk matta nuttape-numꝏ onpenimuneat.

28 Yeuſh n nihyenpaſh ut Bethabara, ong-koue Jordan, nah John adt kutcheſſuſuuudt.

29 Na wonk kefukok John nau Jeſusóh up-peyaónukquoh, kah nꝏwau, nók wuſſambóh God, noh amainuk ummatcheſeonk muttaok.

30 Yeuoh noh anꝏwaomp, nutafub kunk wosketomp, noh miſugkenheau onk neu, pe-wutche na negonuhkunkup.

31 Kah matta nꝏwaheꝏp: aut noh woh wahihau ut Iſrael, newaj peyói kutcheſſum-muónat nippe.

32 *k* Kah John wauwau, nꝏwau, nunnau naſh ouanit, nꝏken wutch keſukqut, onatuh wuskuhwhunaſh, kah uppogiꝏquoh.

33 Kah matta nꝏwaheꝏp; qut noh an-nukque kutchaiſummuonat nippe, noh nan nuttinnuk, noh woh nauadt naſhaueunittꝏh nꝏkettunkquéoh kah uppogiꝏquoh, noh nan

*Ga Kah*

*a* Gen 1. 1.
*b* Col. 1. 16.
*c* Mat. 3. 1.
*d* Heb: 11. 3.
*e* Mat. 1. 16.
*g* 1 Joh 4. 12.
1 Tim 6. 10.
*b* Mat 3. 3.
*i* Mat. 3. 11. Act. 19. 4.
*k* Mat 3. 16.

First page of the Gospel according to St. John
*Courtesy of the Boston Public Library*

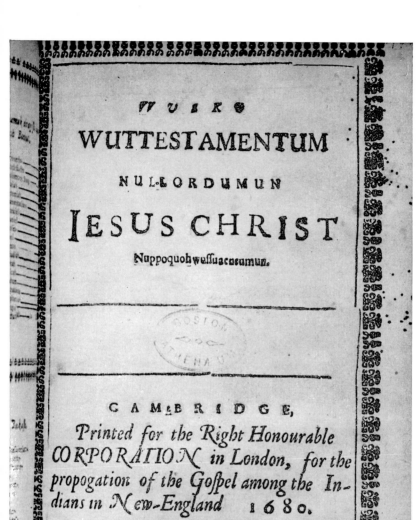

Title page of the New Testament, 1680
*Courtesy of the Boston Public Library*

A letter of John Eliot's to John Cotton, Jr., 1680
*Courtesy of the Massachusetts Historical Society*

*991*

The Chriſtian
# COMMONVVEALTH:
O R,
# The Civil Policy
OF
## The Riſing Kingdom of Jeſus Chriſt.

Written

Before the Interruption of the Government,
by Mr. *John Eliot*, Teacher of the Church
of Chriſt at *Roxbury* in *New-England.*

And

Now Publiſhed ( after his conſent given ) by a Server
of the Seaſon.

*LONDON:*
Printed for *Livewell Chapman*, at the Crown in Popes-
Head-Alley.

Title page of *The Christian Commonwealth*
*Courtesy of the Boston Public Library*

The parish tomb, Roxbury, Massachusetts,
where John Eliot is buried

power to collect money, acquire land and make suitable investments, the full proceeds from all sources to be sent to the commissioners of the United Colonies in New England, who would be empowered to disburse all monies for the purpose of Christianizing the Indians of New England. As a beginning, Parliament authorized a collection from house to house in every parish in England and Wales to further this work that John Eliot had begun. The corporation, later known by a shorter name, The New England Company, financed missionary work among the Indians for a hundred and twenty years. When the company's charter became invalid at the Revolution, the society was rechartered by Charles II and its activities transferred to Canada, where it still lives and carries on the work as originally designed. This was the first Protestant Missionary Society, and the continuance of its work for the same cause through more than three centuries is no small part of its distinction. Self-perpetuating, its leadership through its many changes has sometimes changed the emphasis of its benefactions, but the original purpose has been held to resolutely.[7]

Except for the skill and intelligent persistence of Edward Winslow at the outset in getting the bill drafted and then keeping the interest in it alive through the many postponements of its passage, and particularly in the expert timing of his successive efforts, the corporation might never have come to birth, and without its sponsorship, the missionary work of John Eliot among his neighboring Indians might have ended at its beginning.

The first governor of the society was William Steele, recorder of London, and later Lord Chief Justice of Ireland. The treasurer was Richard Floyd, who served until his death in 1659. The fourteen assistants were wealthy merchants of London. One of them, Thomas Bell, had been a resident of

Roxbury and a parishoner of John Eliot. He became the town's most generous benefactor, particularly in his large gifts to John Eliot for the Roxbury Grammar School.[8] Immediately on formation of the corporation he also saw to it that the £20 gift annually of Lady Armin was added to John Eliot's stipend from the General Court of Massachusetts. His friendship with John Eliot was a continuing source of encouragement and counsel. Edward Hopkins, another assistant, had also lived in New England. He had been governor of Connecticut and one of the commissioners of the United Colonies until he returned to England in 1652. Some of the assistants were less active in the American interest, but all were men of business experience and all were wealthy.

The initial collection of money as authorized by the bill in 1649, calling for a house to house canvas in every parish in England and Wales, went through as planned, although solicitors were not always enthusiastic or efficient. Not all solicited were willing to help, but few residents escaped this knock at their door and heard at least the mention of the cause they were asked to support. Most of the gifts were small, sometimes no more than a sixpence, and there was some active opposition, but totals mounted to the surprise of the most skeptical. The first year £12,000 were collected and invested, and by 1660, it was £15,000. As disbursed by the commissioners, through the years, the income from this fund founded schools for the Indians, clothed Indian children, provided tools and implements as they were requested, paid the sums allowed to native teachers, added small stipends to the native assistants in the missionary work of the Mayhew family on the Cape as well as John Eliot's. One of the largest expenditures was the printing of the Indian Bible, which meant a printing press, type, paper, everything a book requires. The fund also made it possible to print all of John Eliot's other translations. The brick building at Harvard, known as the Indian College, later the printing office, was built and equipped out of it, and the tuition of Indian students paid. Amounts were small, but the list of them is long.

Perhaps more important, through this society John Eliot enjoyed more sympathetic understanding, more friendly association than through any other channel during his entire lifetime. The commissioners of the United Colonies in Boston were often sharply critical of him, annoyed at the persistence of his demands for more money to pay his helpers, to clothe more children, feed this and that needy one, open a new school or reimburse him after he had taken the money from his own allowance because of their delay or unwillingness in sending it. Sometimes the company's treasurer in London was annoyed at him too, for John Eliot was a poor keeper of records. His answers to direct business questions were expressed in general rather than precise figures, and his long postponement of reply was more than irritating to a financier who must have meticulous reports, systematically kept. Most of all, they were annoyed by the many gifts sent to him privately by those concerned with the work he was doing but either reluctant or careless about sending them through the society. What sums had he received from this source, the treasurer would ask him. "Considerable sums," John Eliot would answer. Usually, however, they forgave him for his vagueness and merely tried again. They believed in what he was doing and honored him for his zeal. One letter from the company to the commissioners after one such annoyance is typical. It was written in February, 1653/4. "We are far from Justifying Mr. Eliot in his Turbulent and clamorous proceedings, but the best of God's servants have their failings, and as such we look upon him."[9]

At this point of annoyance, they doubled his salary.

Henceforth he received £50 from them annually. A goodly share of it was used by him, as they knew, for the work with the Indians instead of for himself and his chargeable family. The General Court was paying him £20, the annuity from Lady Armin. Little enough for his needs and never enough for his charities. Once, so the story goes, when the Roxbury deacon presented him with the monthly salary, hopefully secure in a handkerchief tied with many hard knots, John Eliot on his way home, called upon a needy widow of his flock. Moved to sympathy, and failing to extract a coin for her from the stubborn lump, he handed it to her, knots and all, saying, "Sister, I think the Lord meant it all for you." Such was John Eliot.

Sympathy for missionary work with the Indians was not generous in New England and was growing less so with every year. Skepticism was widespread. It was skepticism largely of Indian capacity for Christianization and annoyance at what seemed a blind zeal on John Eliot's part. One can understand both the English and the New England attitudes. The English were far away. They did not know actual flesh and blood Indians or the magnitude of the task to put them even decently on the way toward civilization. John Eliot knew that this would be a long evolutionary process, but he said little about that and was willing to start them on the new way. His New England contemporaries knew Indians at close hand, during the long periods between preaching days. They knew them at too close range to be able to see them in long perspective. To settlers in nearby towns and villages they were often unruly, often troublesome and always in the way.

It is perhaps harder for modern America to understand John Eliot's utter zealousness on their behalf. He was a dedicated man and had the dedicated man's blindness. His zeal was untempered by the layman's good sense. He did not see what the layman saw. He had the zealot's unawareness. Otherwise, very probably, no generation except his own, and that sparingly, would ever have heard of John Eliot. Among the various clues to his quality, his letters to the company, especially those to Robert Boyle, governor from 1661 to 1689,[10] give hints of his inner drives, compulsive and unceasing, and of the undoubting certainty of his conviction. Fortunately for his own personal comfort, Robert Boyle's understanding of these drives and convictions, and his recognition of the man thus revealed to him, were also a spur to John Eliot's amazing continuance in such exacting work. Robert Boyle also seems to have had the imagination to sense the probable influence of John Eliot's work far beyond his own life span.

His association with the New England Company for the forty years he lived after its incorporation also gave John Eliot his best chance to be known beyond his Roxbury neighborhood. Every solicitor's knock in 1649 had brought his name to another house in England and Wales. Some among the first contributors were led to read one of the tracts about work among the Indians. Immediately forgotten by thousands, of course, the name of the missionary was remembered by a few. One can find it in many seventeenth-century letters, several times in the London press, in the communications Edward Winslow authorized sent to the universities and in various other informational materials which circulated widely at the time. Even in England today, after these many generations, a surprising number of English men and women still identify the man and his work. "Oh yes, Apostle to the Indians," they say, paying an unknowing tribute, no doubt to the selfless ardor of Edward Winslow, and most deservedly to the New England Company, which did more than any other agency to put the name of John Eliot in remembrance.

## NATICK, FIRST
## OF THE PRAYING TOWNS

L ONG BEFORE the Society for the Propagation of the Gospel
came into existence, John Eliot was making larger plans.
In his thought as well as that of New England magistrates,
clergy, possibly also of the majority of freemen, civilization of
the Indian could best be accomplished, not by cohabitation
with the English, but in separate towns governed locally by
themselves. These towns must not be close to English towns;
in other words, segregation as nearly complete as possible. Already it was apparent both to John Eliot and to the English
settlers of the Boston region, that the area around Waban's
wigwam was too close to Massachusetts Bay's rapidly growing
center of population. Waban's settlement was growing rapidly too. There were new wigwams every fortnight in response to the General Court's grant widening the Indian
bounds, as Waban had requested. English residents in the
narrowing margin beyond their lands were uneasy because of
this growth. Protest was already becoming articulate. Clearly
this was not the place to build an Indian town.

A similar uneasiness was also beginning to be felt in other
parts of the colony. Two different theories of land possession
were in part responsible, dating from the beginning of English colonization. To the English, the king's grant of a parcel
of land had been the first step toward settlement. Boundaries
had been set down, loosely to be sure, in the charter. The
king's right to grant the land was based on early discovery by
English mariners, by virtue of which the whole territory of

America belonged to the crown. The right to possession, or *civil* right, carried with it the obligation to settle on the land and to improve it by cultivation. The right of the Indian, as the English saw it, was a *natural* right; he roved over the land freely, but did not use or improve it in any way. As John Winthrop phrased it, "That which is common to all is proper to none."[1] Such was the Indian's *natural* right.

In the beginning, the Indians had *sold* land, as they thought, to each new settlement, named a price in wampum and received what they asked. In Indian thought this was sale and purchase, a business transaction, not a mere courtesy. Immediately, however, the lands were fenced by their English purchasers, and the Indian could no longer rove over them as men of his tribe had done for generations. Ownership in the English sense of exclusive possession and privilege was an enigma to the Indian. Punishment for trespass was even more so. Voted by an English court, according to an English concept of justice, it left the Indian helpless. He did not understand.

Moreover, sawmills and cornmills built along the rivers polluted the streams and spoiled them for fishing. The deer went farther away. Indian ways of life were modified by these changes, until gradually, resentfully, Indians began to realize their subservience to the white man, in the land situation more than in any other. Now after some twenty-six years since the first Plymouth settlers came, as a new generation was growing up in the wigwams, this new relationship was beginning to be accepted as beyond change, though still not understood and increasingly resented. Twenty-six years earlier, it would not have been possible for Waban or any other Indian leader to ask white men for land on which to build a town. As English towns became more numerous and extended their boundaries, Indian territory became smaller, Indian tribes felt pinched, and the resentment of white settlers to the nearness of Indians increased the resentment of the Indians. But they had learned that they must ask for the land they had assumed belonged to them as far back as anyone in the tribe could remember. Waban's request to John Eliot on his first preaching day around his wigwam is an example. The scribe's report reads, "they desired some more ground to build a Town together, which wee did much like of, promising to speake for them to the Generall Court that they might possess all the compass of that hill, upon which the Wigwams now stood."[2]

Obviously this was not a spontaneous request, but the seizing of an opportunity favorable to the granting of something long desired. John Eliot presented the request promptly, the land was immediately granted, and more Indians began to come at once. A new location must now be found and the town planted farther away. There is no record of any murmuring from the Indians. After all, perhaps they would rather move than stay, as they had done all their nomadic life. Preacher and Indians of his congregation began to search for a new location at once.

As John Eliot tells the story, after considerable time had been spent in this search and he was puzzled where next to turn, he one day dismounted, tied his horse and was praying for God to show him the way. He did this as naturally, his life long, as though he were talking to a next-door neighbor. While he was on his knees, one of his Indians came down the trail and told him he had found a place. "Come," he said, and led his leader to a corner of the Natick territory. It seemed to have everything desirable for a settlement: fertile fields, woods, a river, a chance to grow in all four directions without encroaching on any English settlement. Roughly the six thousand acres which the General Court immediately granted them, included not only the present Natick, but the Wellesleys, Sherborne and Needham. At this date all this territory belonged to the people of Dedham, who by sanction of the General Court, gave it in exchange for the land comprising Deerfield.

By Indian inheritance, it belonged also to the Indian family of Speene, some of whose members were living there at the time of the colony grant to John Eliot's Indians. Immediately John Speene and his Indian brethren agreed to relinquish their rights in favor of this group. They reserved for themselves only the weir they had built in the river for the trapping of fish. This weir (and every river had one) consisted of two stone walls converging toward the point of a V which was left open. At this open point they placed a wide-meshed cage or basket made of twigs fastened to hoops by strips of bark. As the fish swam downstream, many were caught in this cage, called an eelpot. That they might continue to trap fish here in season was the only condition the Speene family imposed, and this privilege was willingly given. After the Indians had come and were setting up their wigwams, John Eliot arranged that members of the Speene family should "give up their right before the Lord" at a public preaching service, as they did. Immediately they selected house lots in the town along with the other Indians. For many years, in fact, until long after John Eliot was dead, members of this family were listed among the residents of Natick.

The first date in the town records, which are scant, is 1650, when Thomas Waban signed a single sheet as town clerk. By this date the town was laid out, the Indians were in residence and building their wigwams. The first public building was also in process of construction. This was a small English dwelling house for the storing of furs, clothing and provisions, with a small room for John Eliot when he was staying overnight, as he sometimes did on one of his biweekly journeys. After the dwelling house came the fort, the meetinghouse and a footbridge connecting the two parts of the town divided by the river. Buildings of the English sort made problems for the Indians, but as John Eliot reported in a letter, he helped them to get started.

> I set them therefore to fall and square timbers, for an house, and when it was ready, I went, and many of them with me, and on their shoulders carried all the timber together, &c. These things they chearfully do; I pay them wages carefully for all such works I set them about, which is a good encouragement to labour.[3]

He was not only the spark of the whole enterprise, the magnet that held the workmen together; he was also the architect and the foreman of the job.

The footbridge made difficulties, as it spanned an eighty-foot riverbed, was arched in the middle nine feet high and had stone abutments on either bank. Partly because of these specifications it was different from most other bridges built by the Indians, and because it was entirely their own work and most of all because it outlasted the spring freshets and stood unbroken for many years, this Natick bridge became the special pride of the Indian residents.

A few of the Indians built replicas of English houses to live in, but they preferred wigwams which they found warmer and more comfortable. Several groups built not on the three streets that had been laid out, but farther away around the ponds in the neighborhood, though they counted themselves residents of the town.

The meetinghouse stood at the center. It was larger than the meetinghouses in many early English towns, twenty-five by fifty, and with twelve feet between the joists. It had two stories, the first for the preaching service and all assemblies and also for the schoolroom, the second for storeroom and John Eliot's room. An English carpenter had helped for two days, probably at the raising of the frame, but otherwise the Indians had built it all themselves. Using a hammer and nails had been something to learn, as there are no nails in wigwams.

With the town laid out, lots chosen, wigwams set up, the dwelling house, the fort and the meetinghouse built, apple trees set out and about a hundred Indians in residence, the next project was government. "How shall the town be governed?" Waban asked. Of course, like all English towns it would be subject to the laws of the colony, but locally it might control its own affairs. Since at that day everything belonging to civilization was according to an English pattern, the expected answer to Waban's question might have been, "By town meeting," which for local affairs was already standard for the towns of the colony. But John Eliot had another idea.

He went back to Jewish precedent and proposed the plan given to Moses by Jethro, his father-in-law, after Moses had led the children of Israel out of the wilderness. Jethro had watched Moses day after day as the people had thronged to him in every matter that required judgment, large affairs and mere trifles. "The thing that thou doest is not good," Jethro said. "Thou wilt surely wear away. Thou art not able to perform it thyself alone." The solution he offered was the choice of one man for every ten of the people who would judge small matters, another for every fifty and still another for every hundred to judge greater matters or bring them to Moses. "So then shalt thou be able to endure," [4] he said. Moses consented and Jethro's plan was adopted.

This method of governance had impressed John Eliot several years earlier and he had made it the subject of a small book, *The Christian Commonwealth*. He had sent the manuscript to England, but the book had not been published. He would hear of this book again, but in 1651 this Indian commonwealth in Natick gave him a chance to try out the method of Jethro. The Indians were a company of twenty-nine families at that date, a small enough number for experiment, about one hundred and forty-five persons. They liked the plan and accordingly chose their rulers of tens, fifties and hundreds, Totherswamp, an elderly man, being the one highest ruler. Waban was one of the rulers of fifty. This choice appears to have been made on August 6, 1651.

A simple enough system perhaps for Indians at this stage of civilization to understand, but far too mild to handle breaches of family loyalty, to curb underlying revenge toward an enemy or bring justice without violence in affairs demanding a life for a life, survival by the knife or arrow. Indians had, by 1651, looked in on English ways of life for a generation, but had changed their ancestral ways not a whit in larger matters. They would not change now, except that the English magistrate would take charge in criminal matters, and the rulers of fifties and hundreds would handle the lesser. At least so it began.

In the following month, September, 1651, the whole company met in a solemn assembly and took a covenant, written by John Eliot, of course, pledging themselves to be God's town. This was not a church covenant, but the pledge of a civil body. John Eliot had read it to them several times previously and had explained what acceptance of it would involve. They had agreed to pledge themselves and had come together on September 24 for that purpose. Translated into English the covenant reads:

We doe give ourselves and our Children to God to be his people. He shall rule us in all our affaires; not onely in our religion and affairs of the Church (these we desire as soone as we can, if God will) but also in all our works and affairs in this world; God shall rule over us, (Isa. 33, 22) The Lord is our Judge; the Lord is our Law giver; the Lord is our King; He will save us. The Wisdome which God hath taught us in his Booke, that shall guide us and direct us in the Way. O Jehovah, teach us wisdome to finde out thy wisdome in thy Scriptures, let the Grace of Christ helpe us, because Christ is the wisdome of God. Send thy spirit into our Hearts, and let it teach us. Lord take us to be thy People, and let us take thee to be our God.[5]

In the preceding five years, John Eliot had met these Indians at two-week intervals with fair regularity. To have fused their purposes into what this pledge asked of them and to make them not only willing but also eager to take it as a town raises questions as to how he had done it and gives hints as to the relationship he had built up with the Indians. Probably the simplest answer and the most nearly correct one is that his friendliness had won them. They knew that he was not sent by anyone. He had come of his own desire to help them and they trusted him. "And now our next work is to prepare them for Church-estate, to which end I doe instruct them," he concluded, as he reported this September 24th meeting.

Natick reports being meager, there is no contemporary account as to how the Mosaic scheme of local government worked. We have only such details as the English scribe thought favorable to the impression he wished to convey to the English of the homeland to whom his report was addressed. From such instances as are mentioned, it would seem that the "small matters" most often brought to the rulers of tens were cases of failure to keep the Ten Commandments, which were emphasized every preaching day, memorized by the children, used for copybook exercises and often publicly repeated at the preaching service. After a few months these Commandments were probably as well known, if not better, than by all ages in English settlements comparable in size. Several of the Commandments were concrete enough for disobedience to be easily recognized, keeping the Sabbath day holy easiest of all. Accordingly, from sunset on Saturday evening to sunset on Sunday, Indians spied on Indians for cases of disobedience. Rulers of tens were kept busy and fines reaped in consequence. Justice Waban on one occasion gave an order to kill a raccoon to supply food for his unexpected Sunday guest. He had broken the Sabbath. An unnamed Indian split a piece of wood to mend his fire on a cold day. He had broken the Sabbath. The interpretation of *work* was pushed as far as it would go and the precise moment of sundown watched on both Saturday and Sunday.

"If my wife doe some work in the house on the night before the Sabbath, and then some work on the Sabbath night, whether is this a sin?"[6] The answer to this puzzle was easy, but some other Commandments gave trouble. How deeply the Indians realized the meaning of any of them, one does not dare to say. No other gods before me; they had other gods, both good and evil, and they did not forget them, although they professed loyalty to John Eliot's God, and meant it. No graven image; tangible images would have helped them to understand, as Catholic missionaries had known since the first missionary met the first Indian. But covet thy neighbor's house; what does it mean, more than one Indian asked in the question period. Obedience to a rule was willingly given, and concreteness of both offense and punishment helped understanding.

One recorded instance of punishment suggests that understanding could go beyond the literal on occasion. This offense does not concern the Ten Commandments, but was disobedience to the Indians' own law against drunkenness. It involved Totherswamp, ruler of hundreds in Natick. Three drunken Indians, hoping to escape their own punishment, made the eleven-year-old son of Totherswamp drunk also. How can your father punish us, they said, since you are drunk too? They kept the boy overnight. On the morrow the Indian rulers tried the case and found the three Indians guilty. Totherswamp testified that he had warned his son of just such a situation and that he was guilty likewise. The three adult offenders were put in the stocks for the stated time and then whipped thirty lashes apiece. The whole town watched. Now what would happen? Would Totherswamp whip his own son? Yes; the boy was put in the stocks for a short time, and then taken to the schoolroom where he was whipped before the whole school. Apparently the Indians were deeply impressed by their ruler's sense of duty. Perhaps some of those who watched might have resolved not to fall again, but sustained victory against drunkenness, even in Natick, was rare indeed.

John Eliot was as resolute as Roger Williams in his insistence that religion was more than conformity to a code of behavior, but he was also practical enough to give the Indians something tangible to hold to in the way of an ideal. He made one plea after another to the General Court in support of the law against selling strong drink to Indians, but when one of his Praying Indians fell, as they often did, he was wise and gentle in rebuke, always giving him another chance. He did not draw a line between sacred and secular, because to him there was no line. Moreover, "I find it absolutely necessary," he said, "to carry on civility with religion." [7] Many times he said it, and if he had reversed the emphasis of this statement and stated, "I find it altogether necessary to carry on religion with civility," he would have spoken as truly. He kept them together. Occasionally the severity of the Indians in punishment had to be modified. They executed it with satisfaction, and it was rich entertainment for the onlookers. Several warrants which are extant testify to Waban's conscientiousness as a town officer. For example,

> You you big constable, quick you catch um, Jeremiah Off-scow; strong you hold um; safe you bring um afore me
> Thomas Waban, Justice peace.

Quick, strong, safe are hopeful adjectives for those charged with keeping order in the community. Another warrant reads, in a case involving drunkenness.

> Tie um all up, and whip um plaintiff and whip um fendant, and whip um witness.

The code of laws for behavior had been made by the Indians and they took their responsibilities seriously.

John Endicott, governor of the colony in 1651, came to Natick one preaching day late in the year, to see for himself what progress was being made. His arrival must have pleased the Indians, for he came impressively with twenty horsemen accompanying him. His letter reporting this inspection tour was written to the governor of the Society for the Propagation of the Gospel and later published. He had been greatly pleased at what he had seen. "The Foundation is laid," he wrote, "and such a one that I verily believe the Gates of Hell shall never prevaile against." He had been particularly surprised by the "exercises" of the young Indians who took part in the service. One of them had prayed for fifteen minutes, and with "such reverence, zeale, good affection, and distinct utterance that I could not but admire it." This same Indian had then taken a text and spoken on it for a half hour, also commendably. The "diligent attention" paid him by his brother Indians, Endicott thought admirable. Also the psalm, lined out by an Indian, was sung "chearfully and prettie tuneable." He concluded his letter, "I rid on purpose thither being distant from my dwelling about thirty-eight, or forty miles, and truly I account it one of the best Journeyes I made these many years."[8]

Governor Endicott was also greatly impressed by the industry and ingenuity of the Indians in their building of the English dwelling house, the fort, the meetinghouse, the bridge. It was still too early for him to see the extensive plans for agriculture springtime would reveal.

John Eliot also knew that all that he had done in planting the town was a mere *foundation*. He called it "breaking the Ice." It is hard to look upon the day of small things with patience enough, he had written, but he had dared to begin. Already he had established a school taught by a young Indian he had taken into his own home and taught to read and write. This was Monequassun, the schoolmaster for years to come. Under his teaching the Natick children and some adults were learning to read and write their own tongue and to speak and understand English. Gradually the older generation would become to some extent bilingual. On preaching days the whole congregation appeared in English clothes. The men had cut their hair. The children were no longer half-naked. "You can hardly tell them from the English," John Eliot had remarked pridefully, as he described his congregation.

In his view Christianization meant not only becoming civilized, but civilized according to English ways, English houses divided into rooms, English clothing, English customs and someday English speech. Under his guidance the Indians were willingly and very quickly giving up their tribal identity, and trying to substitute everything English for what corresponded to it in their own tribal culture. Assimilation of the Indian to the English was, of course, inevitable, as the two races lived side by side. In fact that assimilation had already gone a long way before John Eliot preached his first sermon to Waban's group around his wigwam. His preaching and organization of the Natick life pushed it along at a much faster rate than would have been natural, but in time it would come. Had it ever occurred to him or to any other missionary of his generation and the next, that the Indian might become civilized and also Christianized and still keep something of his tribal identity, the result might have been different, but substitution of English ways of life was made almost a condition of the salvation the missionaries were preaching. Surrender came in response.

To the eyes of the Indian visitors who came by day after day, the town of Natick, as "religion and civility" were changing it, did not look like an Indian town at all. The straight streets, the wooden houses, the meetinghouse (not a wigwam of the chief) at the center, made a pattern utterly strange. Indians using hoes, mattocks, rakes in the garden plot, spinning wheels visible through the doorways, children wearing clothes, the school bell ringing, young braves and old men with short hair, all this was new and strange. On preaching days, when most visitors came, all was stranger still. John Eliot looked with different eyes. Gratified as he was by the adoption of English ways, he knew all this was of the surface only. Just a beginning, and even beginnings had to be made over and over.

At this date, 1651, he was forty-seven years old. He would continue to preach at Natick every fortnight of his days, so long as he was able to ride a horse. This first town would be his training center for teachers and preachers for the thirteen towns he would yet establish. From this schoolroom in the meetinghouse a few Indian boys would go further in the school at Roxbury and at Cambridge. Several boys would attempt Harvard, though only one would be a college graduate.[9] By the generosity of the London society cargoes of implements: hoes, rakes, shovels, spades would continue to be sent over for the men, spinning wheels for the women, bolts of English cloth, English household equipment of many sorts to change the old order of life in the wigwam. All this stretched out ahead in 1651, far ahead, but a beginning had been made.

If he could only come oftener, they might do better, he said, and if he might have followed his own desire at this point, he might have given up his Roxbury parish and come here to live, but Roxbury would not hear of that. Besides, he knew that he had five sons to educate, and very soon three of them would be at Harvard at the same time. He would pay their tuition by sides of beef, goat, mutton, apples, beans, strawberries, as the Harvard account books reveal, but that meant the Roxbury farm must continue to produce what was needed. This was the generation when every New England minister was also something of a farmer. These were also the years when the town of Roxbury was growing, the church was growing, families were growing, and as the study of any page in the church book will show, the pastoral duties were growing in proportion. More hours of counsel and training for the children who "took hold of the covenant" in entry after entry, singly and in whole family groups, more counsel with the erring, more ministerial service and in more directions, until it would have been easy to say that the wilderness journeys would no longer be possible.

Instead, and not surprisingly, out of the thought and labor (and John Eliot would also say out of the prayer) by which this first town of Natick had become a fact would come a new vision. Perhaps it had already come. Another door would open; he would walk through it, and though he did not (as he said) ever expect to come to the end of this new way, he would begin. It would lead him to what posterity calls the greatest achievement of his life—the translation of the Bible into the Algonquian language.

## THE INDIAN BIBLE

To JOHN ELIOT the Bible was in all literalness God's Book. From the story of the creation of the world in six days and God's resting on the seventh day to John's vision of the river of life, clear as crystal, proceeding out of the throne of God and of the Lamb, every verse in every chapter spoke truth, absolute and incontrovertible. The Bible was the answer to man's questions, whatever they might be. It was the Word of Life.

"How do I get to heaven?" a frightened Indian asked in the question period at the end of a sermon in which he had heard of heaven and hell for the first time. "Pray; read the Bible," John Eliot answered. Not once only, but perhaps a hundred times, after a hundred sermons, this question or one very much like it would come. "Pray; read the Bible," would always be the answer. Yes, they could pray, but read the Bible?

Translating this great book of answers into the Algonquian language became a purpose with John Eliot soon perhaps after he began to speak the native language with some degree of ease himself, perhaps intensified by a look in Indian faces at some moment in the sermon when he saw that they understood what he was saying; perhaps by the chorus of children's voices answering the question he had asked them in the catechism. Whatever and whenever it was, the realization that the curtain of language could be drawn aside must have been a memorable moment.

His own first translations of the smaller catechism, the

Lord's Prayer, the Ten Commandments, made with the help of Cockenoe, came early in his study of the language. In 1649, nearly three years after he had preached his first sermon at Waban's wigwam, he wrote to Edward Winslow, then in London, about the urgent need for schools in the Indian society, if we would promote "this great Indian work for future times."

> I do very much desire (he added) to translate some parts of the Scriptures into their language, and to print some Primer in their language wherein to initiate and teach them to read . . . Such a thing will be troublesome and chargeable, and I have not means of my own for it.[1]

This letter was written before the Society for the Propagation of the Gospel had been authorized by Parliament, but even after he had received assurance of help from it, he still had no thought of attempting more than a few portions of the Bible. Well after he had made a start, he wrote to Thomas Thorowgood in 1653:

> I have had a great longing desire (if it be the will of God) that our Indian language might be sanctified by the translation of the holy Scriptures into it . . . but I fear it will not be obtained in my dayes. I cannot stick to the work, because of my necessary attendance to my ministrie in Roxbury, and among the Indians at sundry places . . .[2]

No wonder in that; it was a colossal task.

One thinks of the King James Version. For a thousand years before its publication in 1611, only ten translations had been made, one for each century. Then came the day when the learned Puritan Dr. John Rainholds addressed King James, newly come to the throne, in a conference at Hampton

Court palace, with these words: "May your Majesty be pleased to direct that the Bible be now translated, such versions as are extant not answering to the original." [3] His words provoked opposition from the Bishop of London and an immediate rebuke to them both in the King's slurring remark about the Geneva translation, then in use throughout Protestant England. But Dr. Rainholds' proposal did not die in that rebuke. Persistent political shrewdness presently won the royal permission and the consequent order that a new version be made. The result was what many thousands of English-speaking men and women regard as the most beautiful piece of writing in the literature of the world.

King James first made search for learned men to carry out the plan. After a year and a half he chose fifty-four scholars and appointed them to the task. Other men also made contributions. These translators gave three years to study and preparation before beginning the translation. In 1611, seven years from the day of Dr. Rainholds' suggestion, the King's printer had completed the publication of the book the world knows as the King James Version.

The learned men had translated it from the ancient languages in which they were experienced scholars, into the language to which they had been born. Now a little less than fifty years later, John Eliot purposed to translate it from the English into a savage language which he could use only stumblingly. His helper was a young Indian whose control of his own language was limited to his everyday native life. Translation requires control of two languages, not one, and each of these men was a novice in one of the languages involved. John Eliot was carrying on the work of his pastorate, making preaching trips once a week to the Indians and organizing Indian towns. Except for a few months in 1656, when he was unable either to preach in his own pulpit or to travel, because of sciatica, he had no extended leisure for study, and yet in fourteen years, he accomplished what the fifty-four men had done in seven; his translation was finished and the full Bible printed. This was in 1663. His achievement in sheer patience and self-discipline ranks high and in linguistic ability apparently needs no apology. He had attempted an accurate translation, not a work of art. In his own thought, it was "a sacred and holy work, to be regarded with much fear, care and reverence." The Bible was God's Book and the Indians must have it.

Without doubt his missionary work was greatly helped by this book in the wigwams of his Indians. During his long absences, always two weeks from Natick and much longer from the more distant towns in the alternate weeks, the Indians now, as he thought, had God's Book to guide them, and in 1663, when both Testaments came out together, there were Indians in every Praying Town who could read portions of it, adults as well as children.

He had aimed at a strictly literal translation, far easier, of course, than such a version as the King's translators had attempted. The King had enjoined them to avoid a "close" translation, and to aim instead at the spirit and meaning of the original in their own Elizabethan idiom. John Eliot, of course, could not have done that in the Algonquian tongue, even if he had believed a literary translation desirable. Precise accuracy was his goal, and when in all his searching and inquiring he could not find an Algonquian word as suitable equivalent for the word he was translating, he kept the English word of the King James Version. Scrutiny of almost any page in his translation will reveal these English words. Wisely he kept them, else as in one example, frequently culled forth for humorous comment, he would have had the mother of Sisera (Judges 5:28) looking out of the window and crying through *mishanttooan papashpe,* an eelpot, instead of the lattice. His Indian helpers had searched dutifully, and found the word for eelpot, as the nearest equivalent corresponding to his definition of lattice as an openwork barrier made of narrow, thin pieces of wood. Fortunately, he was skeptical of this hopeful synonym, and he let the mother of Sisera cry through the English *lattice.*

Later scholars have found mistakes, as would be inevitable. Forgetting (perhaps) that in Indian morality, chastity is a male virtue, John Eliot sent ten chaste young men out with their lamps to meet the bridegroom in Matthew 25: 1–12. A few other misfits have been pointed out, but on the whole, scholars in savage languages have found little to condemn, much to commend in the translation of a language without written texts of any sort. What the King James translators achieved in capturing the spirit of the Hebrew originals in English imagery and diction, only an Indian could have done for the Algonquian tongue and such an Indian did not exist.

Before the 1663 first edition of the entire Bible had gone through the press, several portions had been separately printed. In June, 1653, John Eliot wrote to Thomas Thorowgood, "I have this winter translated the whole of the Psalms. "in August, 1658," Genesis is printed and we are upon Matthew. Before December, 1658, a few psalms had appeared in meter. No copy of any one of these three editions is extant. Early in 1658, he wrote, "The whole book of God is translated into their own language; it wanteth but revising, transcribing, and printing. Oh, that the Lord would so move, that by some means or other it may be printed." [4]

His prayer was answered, as he would have said, and the Society for the Propagation of the Gospel began to print the New Testament in the fall of 1659. This portion was finished in September, 1661, and the Old Testament begun. Fifteen-hundred copies of the New Testament were separately bound. The Old and New Testaments were bound together in 1663, and in one thousand copies the Psalms in meter were also included. The Psalter alone in five-hundred copies was printed in 1663.

At this seventeenth-century date, John Eliot was probably right in thinking that Christianization of the Indians would have been almost impossible without giving them the Bible in their own tongue. When the second edition was proposed in 1685, there was considerable debate on this point and a third edition was not printed because by that time the Indians were speaking English quite generally. But in 1663, their understanding concerned only the barest everyday exchange. Moreover, the mere possession of a Bible gave them something tangible, talismanic perhaps (since they thought divine power dwelled in tangible objects), before they were able to read for themselves. The Book was a symbol of authority in their midst. It supplied also the strongest incentive toward learning to read. When Indians in the congregation could discover and decipher for themselves the text the preacher had used, this discovery brought a confirmation of all that he had told them.

Learning to read took time, much time, and learning to teach his fellow Indians took more time for the native teacher. It also took energy, imagination, patience, but for those who persevered until the page became alive for them, a new dimension was added to their lives in the wigwam.

As to how well the Indians understood what they read in the Bible or the sermons, we have only their questions to John Eliot after every service. He printed scores of them in his letters to the company, and we wish he had printed more. They reveal the great gulf between preacher and congregation, between English and Indian, and the patient struggle each side took to narrow it.

How doth much sinne make grace abound? [This had been the text.]

What meaneth that, We cannot serve two masters?

What meaneth that of two debtors, one oweth much, the other but little?

What meaneth that, Let the trees of the Wood rejoice?

What meaneth a new heaven and a new earth?

What meaneth lifting up hands to God?

What meaneth blessed are they that mourn?

What is it to eat Christ his flesh and drink his blood? What meaneth it?

What meaneth this That God will not hold him guiltless that taketh his name in vain? [5]

The puzzle is by no means in the translation, but often in the figurative language of the original. A word for word literal translation could make the meaning too dark for comprehension.

They liked the Old Testament stories best of all. Why not? Those stories have won us all: Joseph and the coat of many colors, Gideon and the fleece, the walls of Jericho falling, the children of Israel crossing on dry land, Moses and the burning bush, Samson carrying off the gates of Gaza, Daniel in the lion's den, Elijah in his chariot of fire, David and the giant Goliath, "Absalom, my son, my son." These were real people to them; they knew their stories; they borrowed their names. Noah and Job, Esau and Samuel, Ruth and Naomi, Joshua and Ezra; these Old Testament people created a new world for them. The Indians wanted to know more about them: Why did Abraham buy a place to bury in? Did Abimalech know that Sarah was Abraham's wife? Seeing Eve was the first in sinne, whether did she die first? Few details in the story of these Indians are more revealing than these puzzled questions. Two races, two cultures, two languages, and how to find the bridge across?

The alleged "confessions" made by the Indians as part of the examination to determine their fitness as church members are full of biblical phrases. No doubt many of these came from the sermons they had heard; clearly some came from their own reading of the Bible. Also the Indian "Exercises" spoken by young Indians in training for the ministry and expecting to be sent out to preach in other Indian towns, are often largely biblical quotations. What else could they say?

Through the long process of translating these 1180 pages in the first edition, John Eliot had little encouragement from his own countrymen of New England. Some doubted his ability to make the translation. More doubted the ability of the Indians to understand what he had translated. Still more grew all but completely skeptical of Indian sincerity in conversion. Hugh Peter, minister at Salem, did great damage to the cause by calling the whole missionary scheme a hoax and alleged Indian conversions a mere cheat. Discouragement must have been very near many times for John Eliot, but the stoutness of his own intention to finish the translation, once he saw the end in sight as a possibility, kept him going. As to the value of what he was doing, he had not the dimmest doubt. Over and over he said, "The Bible is the Word of life. They must have it."

More than once he had to defend to the commissioners his claim that the Indians as far south as Connecticut could understand his translation. Proof is hard to come by. The Massachusetts Indian language was changing, as more and more Indians began to use English of a pidgin sort, but change came slowly. Dialectical differences were slight, and many of these were differences in pronunciation, not in spelling of the word. Some of the compounds he used were his own, and though he had followed the practice of an agglutinative language in making them, many of these new compounds may have been strange to the Indian. We have no way of knowing. The carefully phrased verdict of Mr. J. H. Trumbull, a scholar in the Indian languages, is in John Eliot's favor. He writes, "On the whole, his version was probably as good as any *first* version that has been made, from his time to ours, in a previously unwritten and so-called 'barbarous' language." [6]

England was far more hospitable than America, and John Eliot had genuine sympathy from the governor and assistants of the Society for the Propagation of the Gospel, who paid the entire cost of printing. The work was done in Cambridge, Massachusetts, at the printing shop of Samuel Green, the only printer in New England at this time. He owned the only printing press in the colony, originally brought over in 1628 and formerly owned by President Dunster of Harvard. The London society sent over a new press in 1654 for the printing of John Eliot's work, and also several fonts of type, with plentiful *k*'s, *oo*'s, *q*'s, as the Algonquian language would require. In 1660 when the manuscript of the Bible was ready for printing they engaged Marmaduke Johnson, a London printer, to come over on a three-year contract and do the work. He came, and in spite of various interruptions because of his irregular conduct, with consequent orders from the General Court for him to return to England, he stayed and completed the work. Another workman was sent over to bind the books. The completed edition of 1663 was the first Bible to be printed in America.

Twenty-six copies were specially bound, two for King James, one for the Lord Chancellor, one for each of the chancellors of the universities, one for various Englishmen who had been especially interested in this translation. One of these men was Dr. John Rainholds, who had made the suggestion of a new edition of the Bible to King James in 1604.

Other copies were inscribed for Jesus College and Sion College.

Presentation copies to King James were given by Robert Boyle, governor of the London Society for Propagation of the Gospel. Mr. Boyle wrote to John Winthrop, Jr., describing this occasion.

> I waited this day upon the King with your translation of the Bible, which, I hope I need not tell you, he received according to his custom very gratiously. But though he looked a pretty while upon it, & shewed some things in it to those that had the honour to be about him in his bed-chamber, into which he carryd it, yet the unexpected comming in of an Extraordinary Envoye' from the Emperour hindred me from receuing that fuller expression of his grace towards the Translators and Dedicators that might otherwise have been expected.[7]

Any one of the extant copies of this Indian Bible gives eloquent testimony to heavy use. Some pages are so worn and thin and darkened by handling that they can be read only with difficulty. Not an excessively rare book in either the 1663 or the 1685 edition, it has become, understandably enough, a collector's prize. The sale price of $43,000.00 at auction in the Parke Bernet Galleries, May 4, 1966, would have no meaning for John Eliot. He served other gods.

We honor him for the selflessness of his motive in this translation: to bring light to the darkened mind of the Indian. We honor him also for the unsparing discipline by which he persevered until the task was completed. Only an Indian could say to what degree he succeeded. Miles Smith in his preface to the King James Version, wrote, "Translation it is that openeth the window to let in the light; that breaketh the shell, that we may eat the kernel, that putteth aside the curtain, that we may look into the most holy place, that removeth the cover of the well, that we may come by the water."

Maybe there were those among the Praying Indians for whom *Mamusse Wunneetupanatamwe Up-Biblum God* could do just that.

## THE FIRST INDIAN CHURCH

THE INDIAN DESIRE for a church of their own had grown steadily since John Eliot's early sermons at Waban's wigwam. After they had listened to him for a few months and some of their leaders had declared their willingness to "pray to God" (their expression for the Englishman's way of religion), members of his congregation came to him, asked to be baptized and to be allowed to become church members. John Eliot was too wise to let their desire be fulfilled prematurely and he told them that they must first be civilized by being brought together from their wild ways of living. They must "come up into civil Cohabitation, Government and Labor," and have a fixed condition of life before they could be entrusted with the sacred ordinances of church communion. They were disappointed but they accepted his judgment, and after three more years the path to settled living led them to Natick.

After they had arrived there in 1650, and were living in their own homes, had taken the covenant as a town and promised to be God's people, once again "the wiser and better sort of them" renewed the plea, "Let us have a church of our own."

John Eliot gave ear to their plea, and after counsel with brother ministers went ahead with the first step. This was the same step as was always taken with an English group desiring to be organized into a church body. Those desiring membership first gave testimony in public as to their religious experience and purpose. "Confession" was the word for these personal recitals and with the English they were not only spoken publicly, but also presented in writing. No exception would be made with the Indians. John Eliot wrote down each confession, word for word as it was given, and later sent an English translation of all confessions to the neighboring ministers. When these men saw nothing to prevent proceeding further, an assembly was called with these ministers present, their purpose being to "discern the Reality of Grace in these Indians." This assembly was called for October 13, 1652. It was a most solemn occasion.

The confession previously taken from each Indian was first read in translation by John Eliot. This was followed by another impromptu confession, slowly spoken, written down word for word, just as the one previously given had been, and then read in English translation to the assembly.[1] This process took hours, for some of the confessions were pages long, and after each one had been vouched for by the native interpreters present as correctly written down by John Eliot and then correctly translated by him into English, the English ministers present were weary and unwilling to hear all of the candidates. But since they did not understand Algonquian, and were unwilling to take anything for granted, they were obliged to endure the weariness.

Totherswamp, ruler of hundreds in Natick, was the first called. His confession of the day began:

> I confess in the presence of the Lord, before I prayed, many were my sins, not one good word did I speak, not one good thought did I think, not one good action did I doe; I did act all sins, and full was my heart of evil thoughts; . . .

After several pages, it ends:

I confess I deserve Hell, I cannot deliver my self, but I give my Soul and my Flesh to Christ, and I trust my soul with him for he is my Redeemer, and I desire to call upon him while I live.

Mr. Allin, a minister present, asked him how it was with him now as to Repentance, and his answer was:

I am ashamed of all my sins, my heart is broken for them and melteth in me, I am angry with my self for my sins . . . and I desire that they may be pardoned.[2]

Apparently this confession was satisfactory. Not so Waban's, who was called next.

Before I heard of God, and before the English came into this Country, many evil things my heart did work . . . I wished for riches, I wished to be a Witch, I wished to be a Sachem.
When the English taught me, I was angry with them. But a little while agoe, after the great Sikness, I considered what the English do; and I had some desire to do as they do; and after that I began to work as they work.
But I do not know how to confess, and little do I know of Christ; I fear I shall not beleeve a great while, and very slowly. I do not know what grace is in my heart, there is little good in me.
I am ashamed of all I do, and I do repent of my sins; I dislike my sins, yet I do not truly pray to God in my heart . . . I can do nothing, but deserve damnation, I judge I am a sinner, and cannot repent.[3]

He spoke these words with tears and was obviously under great strain of emotion, but the ministers were unmoved by his distress and thought his confession unsatisfactory. John Eliot spoke a tribute to his exemplary behavior, his skill in ruling and the respect in which he was held in the town, but these were not the virtues the assembly was looking for.

The patience and composure of these Indians before this critical assembly; in fact, their willingness to attend at all, is in itself a testimony to the fiber of their purpose. Something comes through in these confessions of John Eliot's teachings in his sermons. Less concrete but present to some degree in every confession and deeply revealing, are hints of a half-savage's new view of himself, his first glimpse perhaps of a different perspective on living. The assembly was not looking for such revelations and there were no anthropologists present.

Monequassun, the Natick schoolmaster, confessed that when he had first heard instructions, he had laughed at them and scorned praying to God. Later, when he felt differently, he had been very unwilling to move to Natick, but he had come. He also found it very hard to cut off his hair, but he had done that too.[4]

Robin Speene confessed that he was ashamed because when taught to pray to God, "I did not take it up. . . . I see my sin, and I need Christ, and now I ask you this question, *What is Redemption?*"[5]

Ephraim confessed that all the days he had lived, he had been in a poor foolish condition. "When I first heard of praying to God, I could not sleep quietly, I was so troubled . . . I think sometimes the word of God is false."[6]

Peter, a ruler of ten, confessed:

God saith, We must have but one Wife, and at first God did make but one man and one woman; but I followed many women. God saith, Remember the Sabbath day to keep it holy; but I did hunt, or shoot, or any thing on the Sabbath day; many other sins I committed, but now I see them, and wil cast them away . . .[7]

Magus confessed:

Heretofore I beleeved not, that God made the world, but I
thought the world was of it self, and all people grew up in the
world of themselves. When any bid me pray to God, I said
I cannot, and none of our Rulers beleeve or pray to God; yet
I went about to seek how to pray to God, I told the wise men
I seek how to pray to God, and all of them could not find how
to pray to God. Afterward I had a desire to pray to God, lest
I should lose my soul, but my heart run away, and I could
not find how to pray to God, and therefore I thought of going away; yet I also thought if I do go away, I shall lose my
ground. But after this I heard of Gods anger against me and
I beleeved it . . . I have been full of lusts, and thefts, &c.
all my life, and all the time I have lived. I have done contrary to the Command of God. And I am now grieved, now
I hear of all my sins: . . . I beleeve that we ought to gather
into a Church, and serve God as long as we live. But I do not
know whether yet God hath pardoned my sins, or not; but I
know Christ, and I know he hath already dyed for me, because I cannot redeem my self.[8]

Another confession, revealing not only the confusion, but
one Indian's way of thinking himself out of it, is Poquanum's.

A great while ago the English would tell me of God, but I
hated it, and would go out of doors, when they so spake unto
me, and I murmured at it. When the Indians first prayed to
God, I did not think there was a God, or that the Bible was
God's Book, but that wise men made it: When some prayed
to God, I went with them, but I did not know God. Afterward my mind was changed thus far, That I desired to be
wise, as others were, but yet I knew nothing of God; yea,
after I prayed to God, I still did think there was no God . . .
I thought we prayed for nothing but that our souls might go

to Heaven . . . But after, when the Children were cate-
chised, and taught the Ten Commandments, I hearkened,
and by them I came to know that there was a God, and that
there was sin against God.[9]

Pomampan confessed:

Before I prayed unto God, I committed all manner of sins;
and when I heard the Catechism, *That God made me,* I did
not beleeve it, because I knew that I sprang from my Father
and Mother, and therefore I despised the word, and therefore
again I did all sins, and I did love them . . .[10]

There is much repetition in these pages of confession. The
Indians use the same words and phrases over and over, sermon phrases, many of them. They express awareness of their
sins, confusion, fear of eternal punishment most of all.
Clearly they are not trying to make a good impression, or
they would have spoken differently, most of them. The elders
saw some hope in some of them, but a church must not be
begun "on a sudden" and they counseled more time, more
instruction. John Eliot seemed neither surprised nor cast
down by this verdict; in fact he welcomed it as giving him a
chance to prepare these candidates better.

The next step came three years later, after more schooling,
more sermons, more private instruction. The difference is
apparent. Not confessions this time, but an examination
publicly of each candidate. John Eliot told his Natick Indians
it would be A Day of Asking Questions, designed to show
what they knew about the things of religion.[11] The most interesting revelation from the more than a hundred questions
offered in sample, is that there is very little doctrine in most
of them. Instead, what do you think, why do you know, why
do you believe what you say you believe? A few of the an-

swers suggest very clearly something more than remembering what has been told them.

One Indian was asked, How do you know the word of God is God's word?

"I believe the word that you teach us was spoken by God," he answered.

Why doe you believe it?

"Therefore I believe it to be the word of God because when we learn it, it teacheth our hearts to be wise and humble."

Another was asked, Doe you love God?

"A little I love God, my heart wanteth wisedome, but I doe desire to love him."

What good things see you in the English?

"I see true love, that our great *Sachems* have not, and that maketh me think that God is the true God."

Whether doe you indeed believe there is a God, Christ, Heaven, Hell, whether have you any doubts concerning these things or no?

"I doe but a little know my owne thoughts, but God thoroughly knoweth my heart, I desire to believe these things, I desire not to be an Hypocrite."

Out of what matter did God make the world?

"Not of anything at all."

Had God any beginning?

"No, but he is ever."

Many hours were spent in the asking and answering of these many questions, until the sun was setting. The elders, without enthusiasm, but with sufficient satisfaction that the Indians had been instructed in the things of religion, offered no further objections to the setting up of a church in Natick.

John Eliot made slow haste, however, knowing not only the sincerity of the Indians in their purposes, but also their need of further nurture, and particularly their need of leaders among themselves to whom the affairs of a church society could be safely committed during his own long absences from them. Accordingly, five more years went by while he attempted to train native teachers and preachers, not only in the body of material they would present from week to week, but also in what he called the art of teaching itself. He met these young Indians on his biweekly visits, prepared his *Logic Primer* for their instruction in methods of study and presentation of material, and as they were able, gave them a share in the public service. At the Sunday service, which was entirely under their charge, they had practice in preaching. Later they were sent out to the other Indian towns he was forming as teachers and preachers.

We have a few samples of these Indian *Exercises,* which John Eliot printed under the title, *A Further Account of the Progresse of the Gospel amongst the Indians of New England.* John Speene, whose confession at first was judged short on some main points, was one of the speakers. He began:

A little I will say, for I can say but little, for I am weak and know but little.

Matt. 9, 14, 15. This is a Parable . . . We are fasting this day, because of the great raine, and great floods, and unseasonable weather, whereby the Lord spoileth our labours . . . This day is therefore a day of Repentance, of fasting, and of mourning. And what are we to doe in this day of fasting? Answ. We must search out our sins, and with hearty Repentance forsake them . . . Againe, another cause of our fasting this day, is to prepare us to make a church of Christ among us, and if you say what must we doe to prepare for Church-estate, I answer we must repent of our sins and make ourselves clean . . . Againe, to prepare for Church-estate, we must pray unto God, to send his Spirit into our hearts . . .

We desire to be baptized by man, and man baptizeth us with water, and that is a sign of Repentance; but we must look for the baptisme of Christ, & he giveth us his Spirit, that is his baptizing. Again, he baptizeth us with fire, and what is that? ans. not outward fire, but spirituall, and it is a similitude, thus: What will fire doe? I answer you all know what fire will do: for when your Tobacco-pipes are filthy, foul, stinking, unfit for your use, you cast them into the fire, and that does not burn them up, but burneth up all their filth, and maketh them clean and sweet, & fit for your use. So our hearts are filthy, and unfit for God's use, but cast our hearts into the word, for there the Spirit is, and then the Spirit of God will burn out all our filth and sin, and make us sweet, and fit for the Lords use.[12]

This sample of Indian knowledge of religious matter, and of some training in presentation of it bears out the truth of the introductory statement prefacing each of these exercises, "A little I'll speak, according to that poor little I know." Measured, however, against what he had started with, these *Exercises* probably explain John Eliot's confidence that he had "broken the Ice," which was all he claimed to have done. Letting them have a church of their own promised further growth and development from this small beginning.

In 1660, fourteen years after that first preaching service at Waban's wigwam, the Church at Natick was gathered according to the English custom. Its members were John Eliot's first converts, Waban among them. These Indians had been more regularly and more frequently under his guidance than any others. During these fourteen years he had met them nearly every fortnight, and many of them had come often to Roxbury to consult with him. He knew them as individuals.

No detailed report of the gathering meeting is extant. It was held on a day of fasting, as was usual for such occasions.

Apparently little different from the weekly preaching service, the taking of the covenant gave the added solemnity appropriate to a gathering. This covenant, written, of course, by John Eliot, was called the *Covenanting Confession*. Only two copies are extant. It is a two column broadside, Indian in one column, English in the other. The date of printing is not known, but the type is the same as that used in the printing of the 1663 edition of the Bible. There is a brief statement of belief in the existence of God, his creation of the world and of man, the sin of Adam, our sin in consequence, God's judgment and salvation through Christ. The covenanting group agreed to this belief, bound themselves to keep the Sabbath, to give their children to Jesus Christ, and to walk with him as a church as long as they lived. Having solemnly taken this covenant as a group, each member having previously been judged fit, the Church at Natick was thereafter regarded as one of the New England churches. No list of the first members is extant.

Fourteen years of John Eliot's thought and life (and prayer) had gone into what this day represented. It was a landmark. He was fifty-six years old, and already, as he had said in a letter two years before, "For my selfe I feel my strength to decay, and I am not able to doe and to bear what I have done, and although temptation may sometime breed waverings, yet my soul doth desire and beleeve, that I shall live and die in the work." [13]

When he wrote this letter he was only recently recovered from a long and painful illness with sciatica, which left him lame for the remainder of his life, but vigor had returned and he was making his weekly journeys as before, most of them much farther from Roxbury. Added responsibilities of mature life in Roxbury, in Boston and on the Cape, made these his busiest, most crowded years, always with more than one day of the week in the saddle. These were also the years in which completion of the translation of the Bible was his dearest hope.

The decade of the 1650's had brought the first break in the Eliot family circle. The fourth son, Aaron, a boy of twelve, just ready to begin his work at Harvard, had died. The eldest son, John, had received his second Harvard degree, was established in his pulpit and, in addition, was preaching regularly to the Indians every fortnight. The second son, Joseph, had taken his first degree at Harvard, was also established in his own pulpit, and had just been accepted by the Society for the Propagation of the Gospel as a preacher to the Indians once a fortnight. Samuel, the third one, taking his A.B. from Harvard in this same year, 1660, would do likewise for the four years he had yet to live. Son John would have only eight more years to live. But these sorrows for John Eliot were still in the future.

As he looked around him in 1660, he rejoiced in the decision of three of his sons to follow him in the work with the Indians. When they were children, he had dedicated them to God (as he said), hoping that they would do just this. He was also encouraged in 1660 by the fact of young Indians training for work in the other Indian towns now being formed. In time, there would be more churches, as at Natick. But he was clear-eyed and realistic as he looked ahead. Not only was he aware that his own strength was failing, but he also knew that he was walking a lonely path.

> So few looke after what we doe, [he had written to Edward Winslow] or doe so much as ask us about it . . . I find recompence enough to my soul in the work it selfe . . . and I humbly blesse the Lord who caryeth my soule above all discouragement.[14]

The establishment of this first church at Natick had been one signal "recompence" to his soul.

He had remarked in a letter to Mr. Steele, governor of the London society, that as he traveled along "for 50 miles riding, all the Indians we met w^th had some savor of the gospel & had at sometime come and heard the Word, and our coming unto them was very gladly accepted." [15]

The leaven was at work.

## MORE PRAYING TOWNS

NATURALLY NATICK, as the first of the Praying Towns, became the model for the thirteen others that would be settled within the next ten or fifteen years. Thirteen more times new groups of Indians would ask many of the same questions after John Eliot's first sermons to them. Thirteen more times he would give hints to these new groups as to laying out the town streets, building the fort and the meetinghouse. As the years went on, more of the Indians would build houses with rooms after the English manner, and there would be fewer wigwams. With less hunting and trapping, cloth instead of the skins of beasts would be used for clothing, and it would be made in English ways: trousers, shirts and coats for the men, skirts for the women. The children would be taught English as well as Indian in the schools, and they would begin to be bilingual. Rulers of tens, fifties, and hundreds would be chosen, young and old would know about Jethro, and always some child would bear his name in the Who's Who of Old Testament Indians in the town. Time after time prayer and hope and labor would become concrete achievement in the establishment of one more Indian town. Count in the early 1670's showed an approximate total of 1100 Indians on the way to be civilized and Christianized in testimony to the fruitful ministry of one man.

Each of the thirteen towns set up after Natick was some distance from Boston, in the now strengthened theory that civilization and religion had a better chance when Indians

and whites lived separately. Each town was granted a generous acreage by the General Court. Sites were chosen with a
view to land favorable for agriculture, always with large tracts
of woodland, a river or lake for fishing, and, if possible, some
encouragement to a special industry.

Daniel Gookin, magistrate, was made superintendent of all
these Indian towns in 1656, and held courts regularly in them
to deal with matters beyond local control. In 1674, when all
fourteen had been planted, with still others in prospect, he
printed a pamphlet entitled *Historical Collections of the Indians in New England.* Knowing each town through all of its
history during his own twenty years of service, he could speak
with authority and give to each some hint of individual-
ity. He discussed them in the order of their founding.[1]

Of Natick he added a few details which give some color to
the picture. On Sunday the Indians assemble twice at the beat
of the drum, and walk solemnly to the meetinghouse, dressed
in their English best. On the bare benches inside the men sit
on one side, the women on the other, precisely as in English
practice, even to "age, quality, and degree, in a comely manner." We see Waban, now grown old, paid a tribute for his
prudence and piety. "I do not know of any Indian that excels
him," Gookin adds.

Pakenit, or Punkapaog, was the next town after Natick.
Fourteen miles south of Boston, it had a territory of eight
thousand acres, twelve families, or approximately sixty Indians. They had come from Neponset Mill, one of John Eliot's
first preaching posts, and his first thought had been to take
them to Natick with the Nonantum Indians. They had been
unwilling to move there, however, and he had formed them
into a town at their first settlement site. In addition to farm-
ing, keeping cattle and swine, these Punkapaog Indians made
cedar shingles and clapboards from a cedar swamp within

their bounds. These proved to be a most marketable product, and in so far as they were industrious, the Indians prospered. It was at this town that John Eliot, Jr., preached until his death in 1668.[2]

Hassanamasitt, meaning a place of small stones, now Grafton, was thirty-eight miles from Boston. It also had eight thousand acres, and approximately sixty Indians. The twelve families who lived here farmed with more success than residents of any other Indian town of its size. They kept cattle and swine and marketed fruit from the orchards they had set out, mainly apple orchards. The second Indian church was gathered here in 1671. "This is a hopeful plantation," Daniel Gookin reported. The Indian pastor, trained at Natick, was Tackuppwillin, and the ruling elder was Piambow. Printer James, invaluable in the printing of the Indian Bible, lived here, proudly attaching his trade to his name.[3]

Okommakamesit, now Marlborough, with ten families, was thirty miles west of Boston, and though it had six thousand acres of good land, it proved to be too close to the English town then called Marlborough for the contentment and prosperity of either Indians or English. Restlessness, friction, and improvidence were also enemies to the growth of religion here.[4]

Wamesitt, twenty miles northwest of Boston, with two thousand five hundred acres and the conjunction of two rivers, the Merrimack and the Concord, was an excellent fishing place which drew many "strange Indians" at the fishing seasons. They were non-praying Indians, and their coming and going, their ridicule of Sunday keeping, their inhospitality to civilized ways of living, brought temptation. The natural resources of the location, giving the resident Indians a better chance to prosper than in the other Indian towns, also made life easier, and the Indians grew indolent. Religion did not flourish here, Gookin thought, because of the strange Indians constantly disturbing the surfaces of life.

On the keeping of the court day in 1674, when John Eliot had accompanied Gookin, Wannalancet, son of the fabled Passaconaway, stood up in meeting after John Eliot's sermon, and announced that he would become a Christian. His speech is worth quoting.

> Sir, you have been pleased for four years past, in your abundant love, to apply yourselves particularly unto me and my people, to exhort, press and persuade us to pray to God. I am very thankful to you for your pains. I must acknowledge, I have, all my days, used to pass in an old canoe, and now you exhort me to change and leave my old canoe, and embark in a new canoe, to which I have hitherto been unwilling: but now I yield myself to your advice, and enter into a new canoe, and do engage to pray to God hereafter.

The natural imagery of his race enters into this direct statement of purpose. His purpose carried a penalty, however, as was often true for the Praying Indians, as Christianity created a gulf between them and their own brethren. Henceforth many of Wannalancet's people deserted him as a ruler of the tribe. According to later report, however, he persevered, came to meeting, and kept the Sabbath (the current test, as his people saw it). During King Philip's War, he and many of his people fled into hiding, remained in secluded territory and took no part in the fighting.[5]

Nashobah, now Littleton, twenty-five miles from Boston with eight thousand acres, was a place of apple orchards from which the Indians made cider, with consequent drunkenness as the chief problem for both missionary and magistrate. Laws forbidding the English to sell strong drink to Indians were constantly disobeyed; moreover, as soon as they took on settled living, the Indians sowed barley and planted apple orchards as a source of their own strong drink.[6] To some degree, every Indian town faced this problem.

Magunkaquog, seventh of the Old Praying Towns, so named as a place of great trees, was twenty-four miles from Boston and had eleven families, most of whom attended meeting at Natick. Their teacher was Job.[7]

In addition to the seven Old Towns, there were also seven New Praying Towns in the Nipmuck country, all of which John Eliot and Daniel Gookin visited together on the 1674 journey. These towns were farther away and not yet fully established. Manchage, of twelve families, Chabanakongkowun, with nine, the home of Black James, constable of all the Praying Towns, Maanexit, sixty miles from Boston with twenty families, Quantisset, seventy-four miles, also with twenty families and land so fertile the residents boasted of their forty bushels of corn to the acre. Daniel, trained at Natick, was their minister.

At Wabquissit, seventy-two miles from Boston, near the southern line of Massachusetts, when John Eliot was holding a meeting on his journey with Daniel Gookin in 1674, an agent of Uncas, Sachem of the Mohicans, was present. He sat silent through the sermon, then rose and spoke, saying, "Uncas is not well pleased, that the English should pass over Mohegan River, to call his Indians to pray to God." [8]

John Eliot answered that it was his work to call upon all men everywhere to repent and embrace the Gospel, but that he did not meddle with civil right or jurisdiction. Magistrate Gookin supported him, reminding the assembly that the English took no tribute from them, nor taxed them, nor interfered with the rights of the sachems in any way. For the most part, John Eliot's opponents in his work and his most severe critics were English settlers, but occasionally, as on this day, there were hints of a solid front of opposition from the Indians just beyond the river. The Indians of Uncas were near enough to offer many hindrances to whatever John Eliot should try to do for the hundred and fifty settlers in this, his latest town.

At this date, 1674, other new towns were in the process of being settled at this far outpost. Daniel Gookin mentions two more, Weskakin and Quabaugh, also in the Nipmuck country, too far away for John Eliot to visit often, but in Gookin's report, "coming on to receive the Gospel."

During the twenty-five year span, 1650–1675, during which John Eliot's fourteen towns were being settled and beginning to act as leaven in the lump of Indian population in Massachusetts, other English missionaries were also at work all over New England. Of these the Mayhew family on the islands were the most successful, topping in numbers John Eliot's alleged Christianized Indians by many hundred. Thomas Mayhew, founder of the family, was a Southampton merchant, who came to America in 1631, the same year as John Eliot. Having purchased Indian rights on the islands, he became successfully patentee, governor, chief justice and remained a resident for the remainder of his life. After his minister son, Thomas Jr., was lost at sea in 1657, he attempted to carry on the missionary work until his own death. His grandson Experience and Experience's son and grandson continued the work for two more generations, making a total for the family of a hundred and sixty-three years of teaching, preaching and founding Indian towns in the long story of missionary work in New England. John Eliot's association, especially with Thomas Mayhew, his own contemporary, was understanding and sympathetic, none more so. He once wrote of the Mayhew family: "If any of the human race ever enjoyed the luxury of doing good, if any Christian ever could declare what it is to have peace, not as the world gives, but which surpasses the conception of those who look not beyond the world, we may believe this was the happiness of the Mayhews." [10] Because of the protection and isolation of the island situation, the Indians trained under this family's nurture were spared some of the temptations of the mainland towns. In King Philip's War they suffered no hardships such as came to John Eliot's converts.

In addition to the Mayhews, there was also John Cotton of Plymouth, who helped John Eliot somewhat in his revision of the Indian Bible, James Fitch and Abraham Pierson in Connecticut, Richard Bourne of Sandwich, Richard, Ezra and Joseph Browne at Mashpee, three generations of Tuppers at Sandwich, serving the church in their town for a hundred and twenty-nine years, and Samuel Treat, who preached to the Indians for forty-five years. The London Society for the Propagation of the Gospel was helping generously with all of this work.

By the 1670's when John Eliot made his trip with Daniel Gookin to all of his fourteen towns, the missionary work both in the islands and on the mainland was moving slowly but steadily forward. The foundations seemed secure, and the outlook hopeful, in spite of criticism and deep distrust in many quarters. In concluding his account of the 1674 visit, Daniel Gookin wrote, "The harvest is ripe for many more [towns], if God please to thrust forth labourers." [11]

But instead of that harvest, in the following year came the war with King Philip, after which John Eliot's work of more than thirty years lay in ruins.

## THE PRAYING INDIANS
## IN KING PHILIP'S WAR

IN TERMS OF THE TOWNS that were destroyed, the numbers of
their people killed, sold into slavery in the West Indies or
dead from exposure and disease, it is easy to see that King
Philip's War left only fragments of what John Eliot's thirty
years of labor for the Massachusetts Indians had accomplished. Such devastation is indeed the fact. Of the fourteen
towns he had established, only four were rebuilt and resettled
after the war. Members of the surviving Indian population
are hard to estimate. The figure of eleven hundred Praying
Indians at the outset of the war in his fourteen towns was not
reached again during the fourteen years he had yet to live.
Reconstruction went vigorously on, and for the mountainous
task he faced, figures tell little of the story. The Indians on
the islands, protected from the strains of war, showed growth
even during the warring years. All totals are largely conjec-
tural, but four thousand Praying Indians for both islands and
mainland in 1675, when war broke out, may approximate the
number. A precise figure may never be known.

In recalling the magnitude of Indian losses, one remembers
also the devastation suffered by the English, which in proportion to the New England population at that time exceeded
that of any other war in our history. The list of larger towns
almost totally destroyed includes thirteen: Brookfield, Dart-
mouth, Deerfield, Groton, Lancaster, Mendon, Middlebor-
ough, Northfield, Simsbury, Warwick, Wickford, Worcester
and Wrentham. Partially destroyed were Marlborough,

Providence, Rehoboth, Scituate, Springfield and Westfield. There was hardly a family in any of the four colonies that had not lost brother, father, husband, son, and often more than one. Many whole families had been wiped out. Small villages, little clusters of houses in every colony were left in ashes.

This was not a war of great battles, strongly fortified positions, companies of soldiers or of Indians. It was a skulking war, in which any bush might conceal an Indian. The whole village might burn, men, women and children might be killed by scores, and no one have seen an Indian. No record of engagements so far as they are known, can give any idea what this war was like. Even the Great Swamp Fight was not a battle at all; it was a holocaust.[1]

Before the English realized that in order to survive, they must skulk also, the English captain had led his men across the bridge, up the hill, into the ravine, just as he had been trained to do. His horse was shot under him, he fell, the men after him, one by one, fell also. Indians were in ambush, behind every rock and tree. In the second year of the war, when it became a skulking war for the English also, and they began to fight in ambush, Indians began to fall, and the toll began to be more nearly even. But total annihilation of the white man seemed an ugly probability until early 1676.

The Praying Indians in an estimated total of four thousand for all of New England, together with possibly an equal number of non-praying but loyal Indians, probably made up about one-fourth of the total Indian population at that date. This one-fourth proved to be a determining element in the defeat of Philip, and this in spite of the whites' distrust of all Indians—a distrust which soon amounted to frenzy. The General Court tried to protect the loyal Indians from civilians, frantic with fear, and from army officers as well, but nothing worked. Hence the harsh solution of the Deer Island exile for the Praying Indians, to which the court was driven in late 1675. Except for this cruel-seeming verdict, few Praying Indians might have escaped death. Also, in removing them beyond the danger of Indian-hating whites, the English deprived themselves of help not to be found within their own ranks. Indians' forest knowledge, their ability to divine the schemes of their brothers and to meet them in kind, their skill in ambush, wherever used, proved of inestimable value. The English postponed its use too long.

It was the murder of Sassamon, a Praying Indian of Natick, that sparked the outbreak of this war, an earlier beginning, as it proved, than Philip had intended. In no sense was Sassamon's death the cause of the war.[2] That cause went back to the arrival of the white man. Two races, one civilized, one savage, could inhabit the same territory only until the mastery of one or the other had been determined, and that time had come.

The central issue in the long slumbering hostility between Indians and English concerned control of the land over which the Indian had roamed at will for generations. He still expected to roam over it, even after he had made little marks on the white man's piece of paper, and to hunt and fish freely as before. But the white man spoiled all that: put up fences, cut trees, planted orchards, built mills, not because he wanted to spoil the land, but because he had a different notion of what it meant to own land and to use it. Bitter situations came one after another, ill will was built up; treaties ended the violence, but the ill will remained.

With the Pequot War in 1637, hostility broke out into open war and after this war a lasting peace was not likely ever to come. The older chieftains sensed the future threat to their existence and counseled their hot-blooded young warriors in vain. Tradition has it that Passaconaway, speaking to an assemblage of his Pennacook people on the supposed occasion of his hundredth birthday, said to them:

> Hearken to the last words of your father and friend. The white men are sons of the morning. The Great Spirit is their Father. His sun shines brightly upon them. Sure as you light the fires, the breath of heaven will turn the fires upon you. Listen to my advice. It is the last I shall ever give you. Remember it and live.[3]

The younger generation did not remember, and war came.

The 1675 finale broke out first around Swansea and Mt. Hope in the territory of Philip's tribe, the Wampanoags, with Philip, son of friendly Massasoit, as the aggressor. Philip was not a great leader, not even of his own tribe. He lacked both the skill to organize a strong campaign and the magnetism to unite tribes half-hostile to each other through preceding generations. In the end his side lost mainly for these two reasons. Philip became the victim of the disunity he could not change.

John Sassamon's murder was premature. He was a Wampanoag who had grown up in Natick, under Christian influences. He had been a promising student in the Natick school, had been enrolled briefly at Harvard, and when still a young man had returned to his own tribe and become Philip's secretary. His ability to speak and write English had made him valuable, and when suddenly he had left Philip and returned to Natick, Philip was resentful. Sassamon professed conversion, was baptised and became a church member. He was very useful to John Eliot, and helped him in the work of translation. He also became schoolmaster in the town. Philip was alarmed. Sassamon knew far too much of Philip's intentions against the English.

As might have been an open secret, his loyalty now belonged to the English. He went to Josiah Winslow, Governor of Plymouth, with the word that war was coming. A few days later his body was found underneath the ice at Assawompsett Pond, near his home. A group of his friends found his hat and gun on the shore of the pond, near the submerged body, which they buried, thinking he had accidentally drowned. When the story of his death reached Governor Winslow he remembered the warning Sassamon had brought and suspected that he had been murdered. The body was exhumed. It contained no water, showing that it had been placed under the ice after his death. The head showed that he had been fatally beaten. When this revelation was noised abroad, another Indian, Patuckson, came forward, claimed to have seen the murder, and named three murderers who were arrested. A trial was held, the three pled innocent, but a jury, half Indian and half white, found them guilty. They were ordered hanged. The rope that swung the third Indian, Pompapaquan, from the gallows broke, and he had enough breath left after he fell to confess himself one of the murderers, although he insisted that he had struck no blow. None the less, after brief respite, he was again hoisted aloft, and this time to his death.

King Philip now had an immediate motive for war — revenge for the execution of the three men of his tribe — and he made the first attack against the frontier town of Swansea. The great war for extinction of either white or red had begun, and punishment for the murderers of a local Praying Indian had been the immediate occasion for the first outbreak. This was in June, 1675. Plymouth colony was shocked and frightened.

Word was sent to Massachusetts colony, their militia was mobilized and soon on march toward Swansea. Plymouth and

Massachusetts Bay, however, were far from being united against a common enemy. They remembered their long disagreement over the boundary line between them and willingness to forget the hard feelings built up through many years came slowly. Not until critical danger to all four colonies could no longer be ignored, did a measure of unity come, and then it was unity in distrust of all Indians.

Thirty years a-growing, the widespread doubts as to the sincerity of the alleged Indian conversions under missionary preaching broke out afresh, and John Eliot, whose work was more directly in the public view than that of the Mayhews on the islands, became the principal target of abuse. In the fever of war excitement, distrust of the Praying Indians was openly spoken. They had almost no defenders except their teacher and friend of Roxbury, Daniel Gookin, the Mayhews on Martha's Vineyard and a few champions among the clergy. Distrust became rage, and all Indians were condemned without distinction between professed Christians or heathen. The outcry was so violent that the General Court was forced to take action. This attitude and the violence it fomented are, of course, entirely understandable. That a battle to the death had begun was apparent to all.

During the first weeks after the attack on Swansea, the council had ordered that "for the security of the English and the Indians in amity with us," they be restrained from their usual hunting and commerce. Their wigwams must be set in one place and no Indian allowed more than a mile from them, unless in company with the English. If caught or killed or in any way injured, "The Council declares we are wholly innocent, their blood be upon their own heads."

Five Indian towns were named as authorized settlements under this order. The Indians were deprived of their guns. Scarcity of food resulted. Then came the harsher order of exile on Deer Island for all Praying Indians, in response to more insistent clamor from English settlers. Before the General Court issued this second order, there were many incidents showing the temper of the English residents. One group of fifteen Indians taken from one of the authorized towns were roped together and brought to John Eliot's house in Roxbury. Immediately thirty Roxbury residents went to the home of Captain Oliver, also in Roxbury, and demanded that he release the Indians so that they might be killed. He had the courage to refuse this demand.

Before Deer Island was named as the place of exile, several other spots on the mainland were considered. But each time the nearest residents rose up en masse and would not have it so. Suspicion increased. Any ill report against a Praying Indian was believed without investigation. Any protest against such suspicion was not only fruitless; it turned the suspicion against the protester. Finally, since there seemed to be no other solution, an order came for the immediate removal of all Praying Indians of Natick to Deer Island, "for their and our security." This order came on October 13, 1675. It read,

> It is ordered, that all the Naticke Indians be forthwith sent for, & disposed of to Deere Island, as the place appointed for their present abode . . . None of the Indians shall presume to goe off the said islande voluntarily, upon paine of death, and it shall be lawfull for the English to destroy those that they shall finde straggling off from the said places of their confinement, unlesse taken off by order of authority, or under an English guard.

On November 3:

> It is ordered that the county Treasurer take care for y<sup>e</sup> provision of those Indians that are sent to Deare Island, so as to

p'vent them perishing by any extremity . . . for want of absolute necessaries . . . and for that end he is to appoint meet p'sons to visit them from time to time.[4]

The order for exile was immediately carried out by Captain Prentiss, who came to Natick, summoned the two hundred men and women living there, and marched them to a spot on the Charles River known as the Pines, where three large boats were waiting. Five or six carts had been provided for those unable to walk. John Eliot met his people there, prayed with them, spoke what comfort he could and bade them farewell. At midnight, the tide being favorable, the boats bore them away, four leagues, or sixteen miles to the island. In John Eliot's words, "Harried away to an Island at half an hour's warning, pore soules in terror y$^e$ left their goods, books, bibles, only some few caryed y$^r$ bibles, the rest were spoyled & they lost."

The landing place was bare and some distance remote from the wooded sections. There was no shelter until wigwams were built, and winter had already come. Much suffering resulted. The winter was unusually hard, "snowdrifts shoulder high." Provisions as ordered by the Court, were slow in coming, and such shellfish as they could find became their chief sustenance while they waited for food shipments. About five hundred Indians were on the island when the Natick company arrived, more were collected from other villages, and not always in a kindly manner. Captain Moseley, known to be a hater of Indians, when sent to Marlborough after another company, tied their hands behind them, connected them by cart rope and drove them to Boston, whence they were sent over to Deer Island.

Several times during the winter, John Eliot and Daniel Gookin went to see the Indians and offer what comfort their friendly concern might bring. Extant records tell little except to mention efforts on their part again and again, for more food, some measure of comfort, medicines, with consequent abuse from the English because of these efforts. One line in the Roxbury church record in John Eliot's hand reads, "The profane Indians p've a sharp rod to the English, & the English p've a very sharp rod to the praying Indians." [5]

It grew sharper as the days went on. Suspicion of disloyalty against a Praying Indian usually ended in only one way — the gallows, as in the case of Captain Tom, an Indian of Natick, against whom there was "a great rage." It was testified that he had been seen at the Sudbury fight and had departed with the conquering Indians. John Eliot was called to the Court, heard Captain Tom's denial of the charge and afterward visited him in prison. "Everything looketh with a sad face," he wrote; "God frowneth." Captain Tom was tried for his life and condemned to be hanged. "I dealt faithfully with him," John Eliot recorded, "to confesse if w're true. . . . I believe he sayth the truth." John Eliot's intercession for him after the sentence was refused. On the day of execution, "I accompany him to his death; On the ladder he lifted up his hands and said I did never lift up hand against the English, nor was I at Sudbury." [6]

This incident and his friendliness to the victim until the last focused criticism on John Eliot afresh. In spite of continuing abuse, however, even personal danger, he stood firm, though helpless against suspicion and condemnation of all Praying Indians. Once the small boat in which he and Daniel Gookin were riding, en route to the island, was in collision with an English boat, but in spite of strong suspicion otherwise, both men insisted this was purely accidental. John Eliot was thrown into the water but not injured.

He made strong protest against the selling of captive Indians into West Indian slavery. "To sell soules for money seemeth to me a dangerous merchandize," he wrote to both

governor and council, sitting in Boston, July 13, 1675. "I desire the honored Council to pardon my boldnesse . . . cover
my weaknesse, weigh the reason and religion that laboreth in
this great case of conscience." [7]

His petition was not heeded and three months afterward
the seven Indians for whom he made this plea were sold, "To
be transported to any place out of this continent," by the
treasurer of the colony.

These seven Indians were not Praying Indians. "Their ad-
versaries think only how to exterminate them," John Eliot
wrote, commenting on this order.

After the burning of the frontier towns of Medfield and
Lancaster, English violence increased. "Let us go to Deer
Island and kill every Praying Indian," was the cry. The General Court attempted to meet this outcry by recalling the
covenant of allegiance made by the Indians thirty years before, under date of March 8, 1643/4, a document in their
opinion still to be honored.

Gradually, very gradually, during the darkest days of this
murderous war, popular opinion began to be divided, as the
soldiers began to use some of the Praying Indians as messengers and guides through the woods. First only one Indian,
then six, and soon after a much larger number were taken off
the island, given arms and tried out. These Indians removed
their clothing, painted their bodies and became savage Indians again. Their help proved the wisdom of the test through
the desperate months of early 1676. To some degree the anger of the English was abated by the results, and particularly
when the war began to show hope for the English, there began to be a distinction between Praying Indians who were
being used to bring this about, and the savages. But how
could one know whether they would continue to be trust-
worthy?

Testimonials as to their trustworthiness were solicited from some of the army officers who had used them. A certificate from Major Thomas Savage is on file. The first Indian spies had been assigned to him, and his testimony was that they "approved themselves courageous soldiers, and faithful to the English interest." Captain Daniel Richardson, November 29, 1677, reported, "I had experience of the sobriety, courage and fidelity of the generality of those Indians." Samuel Hunting, December 13, 1677, had sent eighty volunteers out at times. They had "behaved themselves courageously and faithfully to the English interest." Daniel Gookin gave them credit for "turning yᵉ balance to yᵉ English side, so that yᵉ enemy went down yᵉ wind amain." Sweeping statement that it is, later judgment by historians seems not to challenge its truth.

The killing of King Philip at Mount Hope on August 12, 1676, marked the beginning of the end of active conflict, but confidence in a settled peace was long in coming. John Eliot blamed himself for declining "to record p'ticular matters," as he had been asked to do, "Now on 2nd thought" [he wrote on April 10, 1677], "I blame myself for it. Lord p'don all my many omissions." We wish that he had written what he knew, for history's sake. He records that the success of the Indian soldiers was "highly acceptable to the English soldiers" but that it had brought a sad aftermath. "Indians are now welcomed wherever met, led to the ordinaries and made to drink." Drunkenness increased, quarreling and fighting followed.

> Prayer to God was quenched. the younger generation being debauched by it, and the good old generation of the first beginners gathered home by death. So yᵗ Satan imp'ved yᵉ op'-tunity to defile, debase, & bring into contempt the whole work of praying to God: a great apostacy defiled us. And yet through grace some stood & doe stand, and the work is on foot to this day, praised be the Lord.[8]

The success of the prewar years would not be repeated.

## A NEW START

FROM MANY ANGLES the situation among the Praying Indians at the end of 1676 called for the leadership of a young man of purpose and abounding energy; John Eliot was seventy-two years old and with failing strength. All of the fourteen towns he had established were sadly devastated, if not in complete ruin. Fire, theft, wanton destruction had left them little more than a shambles. Those most recently founded in the Nipmuck country were totally lost. A few Praying Indians straggled back to the other more remote towns, but the unity and prosperity of their hopeful beginnings were gone. Religious interest as a guiding motive did not reawaken. Workers to help in the cause were harder to find than ever. English zest for the Christianization of the Indian was at a low ebb indeed.

Natick was one of the towns to be rebuilt. It was named immediately as one of four places in which survivors among the Praying Indians would be kept under close supervision for the months immediately following the end of fighting. Fifty Indians returned in November under watch of Captain Andrew Deming. Sixty-two more were held in Newton, twenty-five on Nonantum Hill and twenty-five at Medford, making a total of one hundred and sixty-two. This was thirty-eight less than the number that had marched away into exile a year before. Some of the missing thirty-eight were the aged who had died of hardship on Deer Island. Some of the younger hardier men had been killed in combat. Still others had been corrupted by drink, among these John Speene and

Anthony* who had been native teachers. Most of the number
who returned had kept their religious faith. All needed the
counsels and encouragement of their teacher and friend John
Eliot more than ever, and he was ready to give them.

In spite of his years and increasing feebleness, he was not
one to lose heart now. The spirit of his response to the challenge he faced was that of his letter to Sir William Ashurst of
the New England Company before the war broke out. "I can
do little, yet I am resolved through the grace of Christ, I will
never give over the worke, so long as I have legs to go." [1]
Physically he had never entirely recovered from the lameness
sciatica had brought. "I am lamed, and quite disabled," he
had written to Robert Boyle, but for some years yet he would
still ride a horse and cover the miles.

Specific records of his labors through the immediate post-
war years are almost nonexistent, but from the letters he continued to write the London company, it is apparent that restoration in many ways meant almost beginning over. He set
about to reorganize the schools at once, using the teachers
who had returned and training others who were badly
needed. Supplies for the schools were completely gone. Similarly implements, tools of all sorts, hoes, spades, rakes, everything for cultivation of the soil when spring came again; these
must be ordered once more and then waited for through
many weeks. More urgently, supplies of food and clothing
must be found at once, for another winter was already upon
them. John Eliot was alone in his Roxbury pulpit at this
time and his visits to the Indian towns were brief in consequence, but his guidance and encouragement gave them new
heart for the long, slow progress of reconstruction. Readjust-
ments were manifold and both leader and people faced a sad
period.

To judge from his letters to the London officers of the New

* See his Dying Words, Appendix, 1912.

England Company, it is apparent that to him the loss of nearly all the Indian Bibles he had distributed to the Indians more than ten years before was a handicap almost too serious to face. Without the Bible in their hands, religious teaching lost much of its effectiveness. A few of the Natick Indians had taken their Bibles with them when they had been "harried away" on a half-hour's notice, and now except for a few scattered leaves these were all the congregation possessed. To see them making use of these fragments was deeply distressing to John Eliot. In letter after letter to Robert Boyle he lamented the loss and pled that another edition be printed. "My age makes me importunate [he wrote]. I shall depart joyfully, may I but leave the bible among them, for it is the word of life; and there be some godly souls among them, that live thereby." [2]

However, both the London company and the Boston commissioners opposed him in this plea. They did not regard a second edition necessary, much less as imperative, giving as their reasons, the time required to print it, the expense and the labor of those who might better be working directly with the Indians at this critical time. Most emphatically, they pressed the argument that the time had come when the Indians could use an English Bible. To know English, they felt, was absolutely necessary if the Indians were ever to be civilized. Besides, the terms John Eliot had given in his translation for "the great things of religion" were no more intelligible in Indian than they would be in English. You have English schools among them. Let them read the Bible in English henceforth. Why not?

John Eliot was adamant against these arguments. The charge that his translation was unintelligible to many Indians had been a painful criticism ever since the 1663 edition, and here it was again. His answer was merely to renew his plea.

He had influential English friends and he began to write to them urging them to help by writing the London company in support of his need for a new edition.

One of these friends was Richard Baxter, who had a keen interest in the Indian work and a deep respect for John Eliot. Baxter's reply to the company suggests that he had some question as to the wisdom of a new edition, but he was thinking of a far future rather than the immediate urgency John Eliot was presenting. "If the old man die first," he said, "it is a great doubt whether any will ever perform it. Besides, it may be useful."

Other similar letters presented other points of view, but the company still said no. They did, however, offer a compromise. We will print the New Testament and the Psalms, they said; not the Old Testament. We will also send over a thousand English Bibles at once for immediate use. Their order to the Cambridge press followed this announcement, and Printer James went to work as before.

John Eliot was deeply disappointed and one can understand why. The translation of the whole Bible had been one of the dearest projects of his life. He had spent years of his maturity in achieving it, and now only a few torn fragments were left. Nothing of personal loss, not of time, eyesight, energy or the long patience required had entered into his pleas for a new edition. It was the loss to the Indians. The Old Testament stories and characters meant much to them, as is apparent in the worn early pages in any extant copy. He had often chosen Old Testament texts for his sermons to them, as their questions each preaching day suggest, and as the names of the patriarchs bestowed to their children also testify.

But as the reprinting went forward, John Eliot rode back and forth to Cambridge as before, watching the progress of the work, as the sheets came forth, one a week for his correction. Finally, when the last pages of the Psalms were nearly finished, he took things into his own hands. With a gift unexpectedly received, forty pounds from an English friend, "for the Indian work" he gave order to Printer James to go ahead with the Old Testament. This order was without permission or authorization of any sort from the London company. Forty pounds would not take the printing very far, but at least it would be a beginning. Printer James began to set Genesis.

As charges mounted up with the pile of sheets, John Eliot soon began to have qualms of conscience. At first he told only the Boston commissioners what he had done, and to his surprise won not only their sympathy, but their promise that they would pay the bill if the London company refused. Their letter to Robert Boyle was without criticism of John Eliot for what he called his "hasty venturing." The replying letter from the company brought their permission together with their order that the printing of the Old Testament be completed. The commissioners' letter also informed the company that they were allotting a sum just received as a gift "to the Reverend Mr. Eliot allowing him an additional Sallary to make up a competency for his great pains in so great a service, the fuller reward of which waits for him in another world." He had been using part of his Roxbury salary to pay the printer's bill. John Eliot's letter of apology for his haste humbly expressed also his gratitude for "the love, bounty, and charity" which "still breathe out encouragement unto the work . . . First, I pray, that you would please to accept an apology for my haste. Second . . . that you would please to draw a curtain of love over all my failures, because love will cover a multitude of transgressions." [3]

The second edition was finished in 1685, ending nine years of urgent entreaty, anxiety and of much added labor for John

Eliot. John Cotton, son of Boston's more famous minister of the same name, had given some help toward the revision by supplying lists of new Indian words and making suggestions that elicited warm praise from John Eliot. Essentially, however, this second edition, like the first, was almost entirely John Eliot's work. His jubilation when the work was finished has an undertone of pathos. "Our Indian work yet liveth, praised be God; the bible is come forth, many hundreds bound up, and dispersed to the Indians." [4] *The Practice of Piety* was also finished and ready to be bound. Let us do the Primer and the Catechism again, he added. "I am old, ready to be gone, and desire to leave as many books as I can." [5] This was in a letter to Robert Boyle on August 29, 1686. Two years later, in another, "I am drawing home, and am glad of an opportunity to take my leave of your honour with all thankfulness." [6]

The Bible would not be printed in Algonquian again. When there was talk of a third edition in 1710, twenty years after John Eliot's death, the arguments for use by the Indians of an English Bible were twenty years stronger, and the project was dropped.

The publication of the second edition in 1685 was not only a triumph for John Eliot; it was also a terminus for the active work of his life. He had five more years to live, but his feebleness had greatly increased and he was no longer able to make the long horseback journeys to the Indian towns. In 1682 the company had employed a servant to accompany him, but even then his trips had become infrequent and were soon discontinued. His close friend and missionary colleague Daniel Gookin had died, and now his son Daniel Gookin was preaching once a fortnight to the Natick Indians. He was preaching in English through an interpreter, while he learned the Algonquian language.

On his eightieth birthday John Eliot proposed to his Roxbury people that Nehemiah Walter, who had been ordained
to succeed him, should receive the full salary, and that his
own salary be discontinued. Even walking the short distance
up Meeting House Hill to the beautiful new church structure
built in 1674 had become too much for his feeble strength.
Bunyan's Hill Difficulty it had become indeed. His people
would not hear of this proposal. "Preach and pray when you
can," they said, and continued his salary until the end of his
life. He had made the new start bravely, but his strength was
ebbing away.

He accepted the enforced inactivity with composure and
lived these quiet years with serenity. Personal losses saddened
them deeply. His wife Hanna died in 1687, a woman loved
and honored by the whole community she had served these
many years. There was hardly a household in the town that
did not have cause to thank her for kindly offices gently rendered during her fifty-five years as the pastor's wife. Under
1687 in the church book John Eliot wrote these words, "In y$^e$
yeare my ancient dearly beloved wife dyed, I was sick to
death. but the Lord was pleased to delay me, & keep in my
service w$^h$ was but pure [poor] and weak." Two entries
later, this word: "My son Benjamin was buryd." Benjamin
had lived at home with his parents for some years since his
graduation from Harvard, and had been his father's assistant
in the pulpit. Of the five Eliot sons, the death of Benjamin
left only Joseph, pastor in Guilford, Connecticut, and he
would survive his father by only four years. Hannah, the eldest child and only daughter, after her marriage to Habba-
kuck Glover, had lived in Boston. Her name was still on the
Boston church book in 1687.

Only a few neighborhood details remain to tell us of John
Eliot's last days. It is pleasant to picture him with a group of

Negro and Indian children around his chair as he taught them to read and write. Always a very particular care he had about young children, Cotton Mather would write, and this picture bears out his word.

Many visitors came from far and near, as had been true in all his vigorous years, religious leaders, statesmen, scholars. John Eliot's name had gone far. Wherever his story has been told the coming of one visitor, Father Druillette, a Jesuit missionary who had come in 1650, has been underscored, as though hospitality to a Catholic were worth special emphasis. No wonder, in an age when the pastor of First Church Boston could announce from his pulpit that he would "carry fire in one hand and fagots in the other to burn every Quaker in the world." He also called the Quakers' "inner light" which they professed was their guide, "a stinking vapor from hell." The President of Harvard could also say publicly in those days that "Such a rough thing as a New England Baptist is not to be handled over tenderly." No such words ever came from John Eliot. Instead, he invited Father Druillette to spend the winter as his guest, and though that did not prove to be possible, the two men enjoyed the shorter visit as brothers in the same cause. Neither could speak the other's language, but they conversed in the college Latin of their student days.

In these later years two Labdaist missionaries came to pay a courtesy call. One of them, Jasper Dankers, paid tribute to John Eliot in his Journal, "It seemed as if he were disposed to know us better." Certainly, that was his spirit.

Death ended his loneliness on May 20, 1690, in his eighty-sixth year. There is only one way to finish the record of his earthly story, and that is with the last two words he spoke, "Welcome Joy." They open a vista in two directions.

Samuel Sewall made mention of his death and burial in his *Diary,* under date of Wednesday, May 21, 1690.

Mr. Eliot dies about one in the morning: I visited him as I came from New York; This puts our election in mourning. Friday, May 23. After having sat in Council a while went to Mr. Eliot's funeral; Governour [Simon Bradstreet] and Dept. Governour [Thomas Danforth] &c. there. Bearers. Mr. Allin, Morton, Willard, Fiske, Hobart, Nehem. Thacher, Mr. Torrey and Danforth not there. Mr. Dumer of York there: He comes to ask help; Tis doleful news we have to celebrate Mr. Eliot's funeral with. Casteen is said to head about 70 French, and Indians are above Two Hundred. Capt. Willard came away the very day before the attack.[7]

John Eliot is buried in the Parish Tomb of Roxbury Burial Ground, near the tomb of the Dudley family. This is the Eustis Street burial ground, at the corner of Washington Street. The inscription reads,

Here lie the remains of

JOHN ELIOT

Apostle to the Indians

Ordained over the First Church, Nov. 5, 1632

Died May 20, 1690. Aged LXXXVI.

His latest words about the Indian work were quietly hopeful. In a letter of July 7, 1688, he had written, "The work in general seemeth to my soul to be in and well toward a reviving." When he wrote the *Indian Dialogues* a few years before, he had said, "At first this [m]atter of praying to God was a little thing, like a Cloud in the West of the bigness of a man's hand, but now the Cloud is great and wide, and spreadeth over the whole Country."

The spreading was more than England had hoped when the first charters were written and the first colonists had come. The Macedonian cry pictured on the first seal of the colony had never been the Indian cry. Instead, the confession of Po-

quanum, who said that when the English spoke to him about
God, he was angry, and would go out of doors, is nearer to the
truth of the first response to preaching. The acceptance of
Christianity which John Eliot and his fellow missionaries had
won, had been slow and unspectacular. They had published
the truth of religion as they saw it, and at the time of the
death of these first-generation missionaries, few Indians had
not heard it at some time in their lives. The Massachusetts
Indians were a disappearing race, and second generation
converts were far fewer in numbers, but the work went quietly on. The church at Natick was an Indian church for
twenty-six years longer, until the death of its Indian preacher,
Daniel Tokkowampait in 1716. After that time it became an
English church with the remaining Indians as fellow members.

In other Indian towns and churches, the years brought similar change. English settlers moved in. The town names were
changed, only Natick keeping the Indian name. After a decade or two, few Indians remained. An English church was
gathered, the town was organized, an English pastor called,
and the Praying Indians who were still resident were accepted
as fellow members. The story had had many chapters since
that first preaching meeting around Waban's wigwam in 1646,
and the picture of an English-Indian congregation, seated together, praying together, singing together, is in keeping with
the spirit of John Eliot's fifty-eight-year ministry.

## POSTSCRIPT

I AM but a shrub in the wilderness," John Eliot wrote to Robert Boyle in 1664. At that date he had lived and worked in the New England wilderness for thirty-two years and he would live and work there for twenty-six years longer. When these fifty-eight years were almost over, and he looked back one day over the way he had come, he said, "My Doings! Alas! they have been poor and small and lean doings and I'll be the man who shall throw the first stone at them all."

Self-disparagement did not mean that his share in the work of his life had not been its own reward or that he did not have faith that the dark cloud over the work for the Indians at that time would lift again. He had worked in joy and hope, and he would die in the confidence that others would build on the foundations he had laid. He merely saw the puniness of one man's work against the magnitude of the task.

More than three centuries later it is easy to say that much he tried to do was unwise. Perhaps he tried to do too much too fast. Perhaps the Indians could have been guided toward "civility" without surrendering their racial culture so completely. Perhaps the conviction he emphasized so strongly in his preaching that man's life on earth has eternal consequences might have meant more to them than a concrete heaven and hell.

But one does not read history backwards. John Eliot was a man of the seventeenth century. His certainties are not our certainties (if indeed we have such impregnable certainties to correspond). He took for granted what men and women of the twentieth century cannot take for granted, and then acted accordingly. So do all men in all generations.

To understand him we must remember more than the three centuries of time between his day and ours. We must lay aside the traditional notion of the Puritan, for that pattern does not fit him. He had been trained as a Calvinist, but his teaching of the Indians and his preaching to them do not match that formula either. Neither Puritans nor Calvinists were all of the same cut. He was more realistic than many of his brother ministers in his view of the Indian and yet he did not call him *rubbish* (Richard Mather's word). Always he distinguished between the sin and the sinner. He condemned all that degraded the Indian, the uncleanness, the bestiality, the savagery, but he believed him to be a human soul, a soul in the dark; but the darkness, he thought, could be lightened.

When all allowances have been made for what later times think amiss in his teaching and his multiple efforts toward civilization of the Indian, one comes back to the central principle in all that he tried to do. The human race is one. The Indian is God's own creation. He has the capacity to understand and to be nurtured in things of the spirit. John Eliot went about his task as one dedicated to begin a great work he felt he had been called to do. He believed that one man's efforts can make a difference, and he worked as though he might be that man. He left behind him the evidences of what one man's dedication can mean, not only to a race despised in his day, but also to a nation which is proud to call him one of its founders.

However one looks at John Eliot's story it is a story of paradox. One reads it and is tempted to ask again and again, wherein does human greatness lie? John Eliot was not an intellectual. He was not a statesman. He did not enrich the nation's art in any direction. He was a very simple man. Simple in his acceptance of the Bible as the word of God Himself, simple in his trust that God prospers the endeavors of those who believe that He will prosper them, simple in his assumption that all men, even those who are degraded, are God's children. In this simplicity lay his strength.

There is a phrase in a letter from Plymouth's Elder Brewster and John Robinson to Sir Edwin Sandys, "We verily believe and trust that the Lord is with us . . . and that he will generously prosper our endeavours, *according to the simplicity of our hearts therein.*" John Eliot's strength and authority were according to the simplicity of his heart that God was with him in what he was trying to do for the Indian. His faith was without condition or qualification, and there was power in it.

His own contemporaries would not have chosen him as a man likely to be remembered to later times. "Good Mr. Eliot," they said. They extolled his piety in an age when piety was an ideal for men of great gifts as well as for those less richly endowed. The traditions that have survived about him concern his life as his neighbors saw it from day to day. His lack of concern for his own comfort, his frugality in food and drink, his abounding generosity that could empty his pocket of his last farthing for someone he thought needed it more than he. Not a somber man either, but a man of laughter and wit. But a saint withal. Did he wear a leathern girdle as the saints of far older times? Some thought it must be so.

What posterity remembers — his preaching to the Indians, his establishment of schools wherever he went, his study lined with books almost no one else could read, his establishing of Indian towns, his petitions to the General Court, his translations, although these activities were known — added little to the esteem in which his contemporaries held him. The cause of the Indian was not a popular cause, and John Eliot gave it everything he had. He lived his life on a path on which fame and worldly advantage seldom come. "It is good for the world that such a man has lived," Hawthorne wrote, and who shall contradict him?

Paradoxically again, and in many ways, his life has not only enriched the traditions of America; he also helped to create those traditions. Somehow what he labored to accomplish for the Indian at the very beginning of our nation's life, helped to endow us as a people with the "sense of mission" which is one of the fundamental and most easily recognized character- istics in what we are pleased to call the American character. Not missions in the seventeenth- or eighteenth-century sense of the word, but *mission,* not necessarily religious at all, yet humane, compassionate, benevolent, compelling us (some- times unwisely) to service of manifold sorts for multitudes not of ourselves — building, restoring, training, healing. America's sense of mission is a moving force in response to the world's need. Some of its earliest pages show first- generation men on horseback trails through the wilderness, Printer James setting type, Indian children learning to read.

APPENDIX

LEGACY IN PRINT

NOTES

SELECTED BIBLIOGRAPHY

INDEX

## APPENDIX
## LEGACY IN PRINT

JOHN ELIOT left a considerable shelf of books, but except for a bare two inches of it, they are not in English. In his translation of the Bible and other books into the Algonquian language, his helps for the study of that language, and various texts for the training of his Indian students, he entered and occupied a field in which he stood alone during most of his day and in which he still stands alone among American writers. The more usual fields for seventeenth-century ministers, those of sermons, theological treatises, church polity, chapters of church history, controversial tracts, he seldom entered. Even the Election Sermon he was invited to preach in 1659 appears not to have been printed. He was not a writer at all in the accustomed sense of the word, yet he used his pen toward something to be printed almost every day of his life for over a half century.

*The Christian Commonwealth,* his most sustained piece of writing in English, belongs to the time of his first preaching in Algonquian to the Indians, probably before their move to Natick in 1650. Essentially, the theory of this brief book is that God's children live under a government whose head and ruler is God. Not only the church in which they worship but also the civil state in which they live acknowledges God as ruler. By His laws are they governed and all of them are to be found in the Bible. The word of God is for His people "the only Magna Charta, and no Law, Statute or Judgement is valid, farther than it appeareth to arise from the word of God."

England has a new chance, he asserts, to choose her government, "And as a Christian People should she choose a pattern from the Nations of the World? No. Wisdom therefore it is to look above all such Patterns to find out a Divine Platforme, taught by God himself."

In his preface he speaks by way of apology of his plan for the Indians, that they may be the Lord's people, ruled by Him alone in all things. "This occasion did first put me upon the Study, who am no Statesman, nor acquainted with matters of that nature, but only spend my time in the Study of the holy Book of God." By the Lord's help, he says, he has collected out of the Scriptures a frame of government which he believes to be a "Divine Institution" by which the angels are governed. "Therefore set the crown of England upon the head of Christ; Let him be your Judge . . . your Law-Giver, your King." He then presents what he calls "the scripture Platforme of Government" which he believes will "well suit the present condition of England, Scotland, and Ireland." His plan is based on the advice of Jethro to Moses, by which the people of Israel will choose rulers of tens, fifties and hundreds to rule over them, each ruler passing affairs of larger moment when they are out of his jurisdiction, to the next higher ruler, thence to Moses.

To John Eliot, the Old Testament was concerned not only with far-off times. Jethro's advice to Moses was timeless. It offered a plan for England at her turning of the ways, as well as a plan for his Indians in New England. This is not Puritanism, but John Eliot was no Puritan. The singleness of his loyalty to the letter of the Bible was not narrowness in the ignorant sense. The dimensions of his thought did not concern length and breadth and depth. Back of it, underneath it, animating it was a compelling, unquestioned conviction that apparently nothing could weaken. He was the least visionary of men, but even his highly developed practicality did not touch his loyalty to the letter of the Bible as the guide to life for all men. He followed it to the inch mark, and in this book he is suggesting that the English follow it. He would not have written this book in 1660. This was the thought of more than a decade earlier, quite clearly, it would seem, immediately after the death of Charles I.

He had sent the manuscript of this short book to England at the time of writing it, presumably with hope of publication. It was not published, and there would appear to be no extant correspondence about it. Whether its publication in 1659 was with John Eliot's knowledge or not, is unknown. This was a most unfortunate year for any word against earthly kings to be made public in England, and immediately John Eliot was under strict censure of the General Court of Massachusetts Bay Colony. Colonial relations with the crown at that date were hardly smooth even on the surface, and underneath were currents that could easily lead to explosion. The pages of this short treatise borrowed fire from the highly charged atmosphere and emotional ferment of the moment in the mother country. The situation was highly dangerous.

It was this danger that led the General Court on May 30, 1661, to take action against John Eliot for "sundry passages and expressions" in his book which were "justly offensive & in special relating to kingly government in England." His book was ordered to be immediately suppressed. Before fourteen days had passed, all those having a copy should "on theire perills" either "cancel or deface" it or bring it to the nearest magistrate. Notices to this effect were posted in Boston, Charlestown and Ipswich together with the notice of John Eliot's acknowledgement to the Court of error. His statement was by no means an abject retraction. He wrote, "I do judge myself to have offended. I acknowledge it to be true that monarchy is not only a lawful, but an eminent form of government." All forms of government . . . deduced from Scripture, I acknowledge to be of God . . . and whatsoever in the whole epistle or book is inconsistent therewith, I do at once most cordially disown."

Apparently this statement satisfied the authorities and provided a clearance for him. The destruction of the whole edition by this Court order makes this by no means exciting book a prize for collectors of early Americana. A few copies are extant.

The word "seditious" applied to gentle John Eliot is occasion for a later smile, but this accusation against him has its parallels in any nation's time of crisis.

*The Communion of Churches,* published in 1665, had as its purpose "to propose a way to bring all Christian nations into a Unity of the Faith and Order of the Gospel." There was a far-seeing vision in this purpose, if not in the method by which it was to be realized. John Eliot proposed what he called the "Divine Ordinance of Councils" or a system of theocratic control by a succession of councils, first local, then provincial, then national and then ecumenical, meeting on the first level once a month, then once a quarter, once a year, and then at a longer interval. The ecumenical council would employ the Hebrew language for its deliberations. This is Jethro's scheme all over again, only differently applied. Fortunately it was never tried. But the book was published and apparently bought. Henry Martyn Dexter knew of only two surviving copies in 1880.

Richard Baxter, who had a copy, probably sent him by John Eliot, wrote to John Woodbridge in Connecticut, asking how the idea "taketh." Woodbridge replied, "Truly, Sir, I thinke it better took with himself than with any of his Brethren, not because of his pride, I suppose you know him better, but the peculiar Cut of his Genius."

Baxter's reply was generous and sensible. "I am not for his conceit of founding such synods . . . yet every man may have leave to go his own way in point of unnecessary notions, while they agree in yᵉ same practise." John Eliot's vehemence against wigs shared with Samuel Sewall and other outspoken men of affairs and clergy may be cited as another "unnecessary notion" on which many vain words were expended while the fashion lasted. John Eliot wasted none in print on this vanity, however.

*The Harmony of the Gospels,* published in 1678, was his last book. It brings together the four Gospel accounts, with intention to emphasize Christ's overcoming of suffering. There is also mention of a small book entitled *A Brief Answer to a book by John Norcot against Infant Baptism.*

In 1685, Daniel Gookin, son of the former magistrate to the Indians in the towns John Eliot had founded, collected a few dying speeches of several Indians. John Eliot translated these into

English. As one more evidence that the Indian conversions were sincere and meant changed lives, this little book was widely read for a brief time. These Natick Indians had figured so often in the published reports of the Indian work that readers felt almost acquainted with them. The last word of Waban, John Eliot's first convert, justice of the peace in Natick, town clerk and often spokesman, is a fair example of this repetitious ending. His confession had been rejected by the elders in 1652, but he had persevered, was finally accepted, became a church member, and returned after the Deer Island exile. He was about as old as John Eliot, but died five years earlier. As printed, his last words were these:

> I desire not to be troubled about matters of this world, a little I am troubled . . . do not greatly weep and mourn for me in this world. I give my soul to thee Oh my Redeemer, Jesus Christ Pardon all my sins & deliver me from Hell, and when I dy, Oh help me and receive me.
> In so saying he dyed.

## Old Jacob

> I am neer to death. I have lived long enough. I am about 90 years old. I now desire to dy. In the presence of Christ Oh Lord I commit my soul to thee.

## Anthony

> I was a Teacher. I loved drink. I was often admonished & finally cast out from being a Teacher . . .
> O Lord, save me . . . Send thy angels when I dy, to bring my poor soul to thee, and save my poor sinful soul in thy heavenly kingdom.

## Nehemiah

> I am ready to dy now, but knew not of it when I went out of my dore; I was only going to hunt; but a wicked man hath killed me. I confesse myselfe a sinner . . . O Christ Jesus save me from Hell; Save my soul in heaven, Oh help me, help me.

As John Eliot selected these excerpts for printing, he could recall the long story of the lives these men had lived, from the first high purposes his preaching had inspired, through temptation, failure, confession, another new start perhaps, and now hope, however dim, at the end of the way. No doubt he had a measure of peace in assuming a safe harbor for them at last. They had all been his friends.

These books make a small legacy in English for a long life, but the Indian books crowd the shelf. There are uncertainties about date, and very probably some omissions.

1654  *A Catechism* (no copy found)

1654  *The New Testament* of our Lord and Saviour Jesus Christ (no copy found)

1655  *The Gospel of Matthew* (no copy found)

1658  *A Few Psalms in Metre* (no copy found)

166–  A Covenanting Confession (broadside)

1661  *The New Testament*

1662  *A Catechism* (2nd ed.)

1663  *The Holy Bible,* Old and New Testament

1663  *The Psalms of David* in Metre (2nd ed.)

1663  *The Assembly's Shorter Catechism* (no copy found)

1663  *The Psalter*

1664  Baxter's *Call to the Unconverted*

1665  *Godly Living* Directs a Christian How he may Live to please God (An abridged edition of Baylie's *Practice of Piety*)

1666  *The Indian Grammar Begun*

1669  *The Indian Primer,* or the Way of Training up of our Youth in the Good Knowledge of the Scriptures
To which is prefaced the Indian Covenanting Confession

1671 *Indian Dialogues* for the Instruction in the great sence of Christ

1672 *The Logic Primer* To initiate the Indians in the Knowledge and Rule of Reason

1680 *The Psalms in Metre* (3rd ed.)

1685 *The Holy Bible,* Old and New Testaments

1685 *The Indian Primer* (3rd ed.)

1685 *Godly Living* (2nd ed. of Bayley)

1687 Baxter's *Call* (2nd ed.)

1689 Thomas Shepard's *Sincere Convert and Sound Believer*

### THE ELIOT TRACTS

The Eliot Tracts, as they are commonly called, are the principal contemporary source of our knowledge concerning John Eliot's work among the Indians. He is the author of two of them, and letters from him are included in several others.

1643 *New England's First Fruits,* London, 1643.

1647 *The Day-Breaking, if not the Sun-Rising of the Gospell with the Indians in New England,* London, 1647.

1648 Shepard, Thomas, *The Clear Sun-Shine of the Gospel Breaking Forth upon the Indians in New England,* London, 1648.

1649 Winslow, Edward, *The Glorious Progress of the Gospel, Amongst the Indians in New England,* London, 1649.

1651 Whitfeld, Henry, *The Light appearing more and more towards the perfect Day,* or, A farther Discovery of the present state of the Indians in New-England, London, 1651.

1652 Whitfeld, Henry, *Strength out of Weaknesse;* or a Glorious Manifestation of the further Progresse of the Gospel among the Indians in New-England, London, 1652.

1653  Eliot, John, and Mayhew, Thomas, *Tears of Repentance: Or, a further Narrative of the Progress of the Gospel* Amongst the Indians in New-England, London, 1653.

1655  Eliot, John, *A Late and Further Manifestation of the Progress of the Gospel amongst the Indians in New-England,* London, 1655.

1659  *A Further Accompt of the Progresse of the Gospel amongst the Indians in New England.*

1660  Eliot, John, *A Further Account of the Progresse of the Gospel,* A Selection of the Confessions made by several Indians.

1671  *A Brief Narration of the Progress of the Gospel among the Indians in New England.*

The letters of John Eliot have not been collected. Many are in print, singly, in groups, and in many places. There are a few in manuscript, privately owned, or in research libraries. Undoubtedly others still remain among the papers of John Eliot's English friends. Those in print include letters to the following:

EDWARD WINSLOW:

| | |
|---|---|
| Nov. 13, 1646 | *Mass. Hist. Soc. Coll.,* 3, IV, 87–88. |
| Feb. 2, 1647/8 | "      "      "      "   3, IV, 89–92. |
| Nov. 13, 1649 | "      "      "      "   3, IV, 79–86. |
| Oct. 20, 1651 | *New Eng. Hist. & Gen. Reg.,* XXXVI, 291–294. |

THOMAS SHEPARD:

| | |
|---|---|
| Sept. 24, 1647 | *Mass. Hist. Soc. Coll.,* 3, IV, 49–59. |

HENRY WHITFIELD:

| | |
|---|---|
| July 8, 1649 | "      "      "      "   3, IV, 119–122. |
| Dec. 29, 1649 | "      "      "      "   3, IV, 122–133. |
| Apr. 18, 1650 | "      "      "      "   3, IV, 133–135. |
| Oct. 21, 1650 | "      "      "      "   3, IV, 135–145. |
| Apr. 28, 1651 | "      "      "      "   3, IV, 165–168. |
| Oct. —, 1651 | "      "      "      "   3, IV, 169–175. |

WILLIAM STEELE:

Dec. 6, 1652    *New Eng. Hist. & Gen. Reg.,* XXXVI, 294–297.

THOMAS THOROWGOOD:

Mar. 18, 1653    *Jewes in America,* 1660.
Aug. 27, 1654    "  "  "    1660.
Aug. 16, 1655    "  "  "    1660.

JONATHAN HAMMER:

Aug. 29, 1654    T. N. Veil & Wilberforce Eames, 1915.
c. 1655    Bulletin John Rylands Library, 1919.
c. 1655    "  "  "  "    1919.
c. 1655    "  "  "  "    1919.

RICHARD BAXTER:

Oct. 16, 1656    "  "  "  "    1931, 19–20.
Oct. 7, 1657    "  "  "  "    1931, 22–25.
July 6, 1663    *Reliquiae Baxterianae,* 293–297.
Dec. 10, 1667    Bulletin, John Rylands Library, 1931, 28–31.
Jan. 22, 1667/8    Bulletin, John Rylands Library, 1931,
    "  "  "  "    pp. 31–32.
June 15, 1668    "  "  "  "    pp. 35–38.
Oct. 28, 1668    "  "  "  "    pp. 38–41.
June 20, 1669    "  "  "  "    pp. 49–55.
"  27, 1671    "  "  "  "    pp. 62–63.
May 30, 1682    "  "  "  "    pp. 65–66.

HUMPHREY ATHERTON:

June 4, 1657    *Mass. Hist. Soc. Coll.,* I, II, 9.

RICHARD FLOYD:

Oct. 8, 1657    "  "  "  *Proc.,* XVII, 246.
Dec. 10, 1658    Eliot Tract VIII.
July 5, 1659    "  "  IX.

JOHN ENDICOTT:

Mar. 28, 1661    *Mass. Hist. Soc. Proc.,* III, 312–313.

ROBERT BOYLE:

| | |
|---|---|
| Aug. 26, 1664 | Birch, *Life of Robert Boyle*, 1744, 548. |
| Sept. 6, 1669 | Ford, *Some Correspondence . . .* , 27–30. |
| Sept. 20, 1670 | *Mass. Hist. Soc. Coll.*, 1. III, 177–178. |
| | Birch, *Life of Robert Boyle*, 430–432. |
| Dec. 1, 1671 | *Mass. Hist. Soc. Proc.*, XVII, 251. |
| Dec. 17, 1675 | "    "    "    " XVII, 251–252. |
| Oct. 23, 1677 | *Mass. Hist. Soc. Coll.*, 1, III, 178–179. |
| Nov. 4, 1680 | "    "    "    " 1, III, 179–190. |
| June 17, 1681 | "    "    " *Proc.*, XVII, 253. |
| Mar. 15, 1682/3 | "    "    " *Coll.*, 1, III, 181. |
| June 21, 1683 | Birch, *Life of Robert Boyle*, 439–440. |
| Nov. 27, 1683 | "    "    "    "    " 440–441. |
| Apr. 22, 1684 | "    "    "    "    " 442–447. |
| Aug. 20, 1686 | "    "    "    "    " 447–448. |
| July 7, 1688 | "    "    "    "    " 448–449. |

HENRY ASHURST:

| | |
|---|---|
| Nov. 20, 1670 | *Mass. Hist. Soc. Proc.*, XVII, 246–247. |
| Oct. 1, 1671 | "    "    "    " XVII, 249–50. |

NEW ENGLAND COMMISSIONERS:

| | |
|---|---|
| Sept. 4, 1671 | "    "    "    " XVII, 247–249. |
| Aug. 25, 1665 | *Col. Rec. of Connecticut*, III, 484. |

JOHN WINTHROP, JR.:

| | |
|---|---|
| July 24, 1675 | *Mass. Hist. Soc. Coll.*, 5, I, 424–426. |

Letters to Henry Ashurst, Richard Floyd, some to Robert Boyle, to commissioners, are also printed in Ford, *Some Correspondence between the Governors and Treasurers of the New England Company*, 1657–1714, London, 1896.

# NOTES

### I. INTRODUCTION

1. *Massachusetts Historical Society Collections,* 1st series (1802), Vol. VIII, p. 14.
2. *Ibid.,* Vol. VIII, p. 15.

### II. TWENTY-SEVEN ENGLISH YEARS

1. This entry, with slightly different spelling, is among those collected by Henry F. Waters, *Genealogical Gleanings in England,* Vol. II, p. 910. The Eliot entries, Vol. II, pp. 894–912, appear also in *New England Historical and Genealogical Register,* Vol. XLVIII (1894), pp. 394–404. Dr. Ellsworth Elliot of New York found the marriage record of Bennett and Lettys Eliot and the christening record of John in 1893, in Widford church, England.
2. Waters, Vol. II, pp. 910, 911; *N. E. H. & G. Register,* Vol. XLVIII, pp. 402, 403.
3. A brief account of these proceedings was printed in the *Boston Evening Transcript,* June 16, 1894. A more detailed account had appeared in the *Herts Guardian,* May 26, 1894.
4. William Winters, "Notices of the Pilgrim Fathers, John Eliot and his friends of Nazeing," *Royal Historical Society Transactions* (London, 1882), Vol. X, pp. 267–311. A selection from this article appears in "The Eliot Family," *N. E. H. & G. Register,* Vol. XXXIX, pp. 365–371.
5. Henry F. Waters, Vol. II, pp. 907–910, leans to this possibility, but failed to find definite proof.
6. *N. E. H. & G. Register,* Vol. XXXIX, p. 365.
7. Quoted by Cotton Mather, "The Life of the Renowned John Eliot," *Magnalia Christi Americana* (Hartford, 1820), Vol. I, p. 478.
8. Quoted by Herbert Hensley Henson, *Studies in English Religion in the Seventeenth Century* (New York, 1903), pp. 5–6. For a recent scholarly study of such books, see Helen C. White, *The Tudor Books of Private Devotion* (University of Wisconsin, 1951). Mr. Henson is

quoting from one of them, *Progresse of Piety* (1591, 1596; Parker Reprint, 1847).

9. Richard Greenham, quoted by Christopher Hill, *Society and Puritanism in Pre-Revolutionary England* (London, 1964), p. 443.

10. Foster Watson, *The English Grammar Schools to 1660*, p. 165.

11. For a brief history of Jesus College, see Arthur Gray, *Jesus College* (University of Cambridge, College Series, London, 1902).

12. John Donne, *Anatomy of the World* (London, 1611; Facsimile Reprint 1951), unpaged but approx. 17.

13. For a recent treatment of the English University curriculum, see William T. Costello, *The Scholastic Curriculum at Early Seventeenth-Century Cambridge* (Cambridge, Mass., 1958).

14. Waters, *op. cit.,* Vol. II, pp. 904–906.

15. Cotton Mather in his life of Thomas Hooker, *Magnalia Christi Americana,* Book III, p. 47, says that he has in his possession an account in John Eliot's hand of this school. Early writers on Eliot quote it, but apparently no one else has seen the original sheet.

16. Richard Rogers and Samuel Ward, *Two Elizabethan Puritan Diaries* (Chicago, 1933).

17. The Register of Ordinations by the Bishop of London and also those of the Bishop of Ely do not show his name. Gaps in both of those records may be responsible. His schoolmaster license is also not in the Vicar General's books, but there are gaps in these records for the decade of the 1620's. The statement of Mr. Tedder in the *D. N. B.* that Eliot had taken orders, and of Mr. Venn in *Alumni Cantabrigienses,* that he probably had taken them, keeps one searching.

### III. A PULPIT IN ROXBURY

1. *The History of New England* (commonly called *Winthrop's Journal*), (Boston, 1825), Vol. I, pp. 63–67.

2. Printed entire, *Records of the First Church in Boston,* edited by Richard D. Pierce, *Transactions Colonial Society of Boston,* Historical Introduction, Vol. XXX, p. XVII.

3. *Winthrop's Journal,* Vol. I, p. 93.

4. Walter Eliot Thwing, *History of the First Church in Roxbury* (Boston, 1908), pp. 1–61; "Report of the Record Commissioner," Document 114, *Roxbury Land and Church Records* (Boston, 1881), pp. 71 ff.

5. *Ibid.,* p. 188.

6. *Ibid.*

7. *Ibid.,* pp. 76, 78, 79, 80–81, 83, 84, 182.

8. *Ibid.,* p. 189.

9. *Ibid.,* p. 190.
10. Richard Walden Hale, *Tercentenary History of the Roxbury Latin School* (Cambridge, 1946).
11. *Journal,* Vol. II, p. 215.
12. *Magnalia,* Vol. I, p. 498.
13. *Ibid.,* Article III in life of Eliot, "His way of Preaching," pp. 495–496.
14. *Journal,* Vol. I, p. 151.

## IV. A VOICE AT ANNE HUTCHINSON'S TRIAL

1. Anne Hutchinson's life story has been told many times and variously interpreted. The latest biography, Emery Battis, *Saints and Sectaries* (Chapel Hill, N.C., University of North Carolina Press, 1962), offers new material, presents her story more realistically, and in wider perspective than in earlier accounts.
2. John Winthrop reports this occasion, Vol. I, p. 202.
3. For his mention of court action against this sermon, Vol. I, pp. 214–217, 221–222.
4. For a brief contemporary statement of this gathering, Vol. I, pp. 237–240.
5. A report of the court trial is included in Thomas Hutchinson, *The History of the Colony and Province of Massachusetts Bay,* edited by Lawrence Shaw Mayo, (Cambridge, 1936), Vol. II, Appendix, pp. 366–391. Quoted excerpts are from this account.
6. *Ibid.,* pp. 390, 391.
7. *Records of the Colony of Massachusetts Bay, in New England,* edited by Nathaniel B. Shurtleff (Boston, 1853), Vol. I, 1628–1641, p. 207.
8. A manuscript report of the church trial, copied by Ezra Stiles, and reported to the Massachusetts Historical Society by Franklin B. Dexter, Oct. 11, 1888, is printed in the *M. H. S. Proc.,* 2nd series, 1888, pp. 161–191. This account is the fullest known. Quoted excerpts are taken from it. Mr. Battis, *op. cit.,* quotes from the report as given by Charles Francis Adams, *Antinomianism in the Colony of Massachusetts Bay, 1636–1638* (Boston, 1894). For John Winthrop's mention of her trial and excommunication, see *Journal,* Vol. I, pp. 257–259.

## V. A SHARE IN NEW ENGLAND'S
### FIRST PUBLISHED BOOK

1. *Magnalia,* Book III, p. 41.
2. John Josselyn, *An Account of Two Voyages to New England* (London, 1674), for mention of Francis Quarles. Zoltan Haraszti, *The*

*Enigma of the Bay Psalm Book* (Chicago, 1956), for problems of authorship, Chapter III; Mr. Haraszti also published, as a companion volume, *The Bay Psalm Book*, a Facsimile Reprint of the First Edition of 1640 (Chicago, 1956).

3. Thomas Welde, *The Practices of the Churches in New England* (London, 1645), p. 7.

4. *The Enigma of the Bay Psalm Book,* Chapter III, pp. 19–27.

### VI. "THE PRINCIPAL END OF OUR PLANTATION"

1. In April, 1629, the Company of Massachusetts Bay wrote to Governor Endicott that they were sending the company's seal in silver by Mr. Samuel Sharpe, a passenger in the *George*. A later seal, engraved by John Hull, 1657, passed away with the charter in 1684. For a discussion in some detail, see *M. H. S. Proc.* (1867), Vol. x, pp. 94–104.

2. A translation from the Latin translation made by Casco at Rome and printed there in 1493. Mr. Samuel Eliot Morison offers a fresh translation from the original of the letter of Columbus in his *Christopher Columbus, Mariner* (Boston, 1954), Appendix, pp. 205–213.

3. Of the biographies in English, Francis Augustus MacNutt, *Bartholomew De Las Casas, His Life, His Apostulate, and his Writings* (New York and London, 1909), pp. 287–293, deals with the debate.

4. Quoted by Lewis Hanke, *Aristotle and the American Indian* (Chicago, 1959), p. 112. Mr. Hanke gives a book-long treatment of this debate.

5. Quoted by MacNutt, pp. 291–292.

6. *Hakluytus Posthumus* (Glasgow, 1906), Vol. xviii, Chapter IV, pp. 176–180. "The Summe of the disputation betweene Fryer Bartolomew de las Casas or Casaus, and Doctor Sepulueda."

7. William Symonds, Alexander Brown, *The Genesis of the United States* (Boston and New York, 1890), Vol. i, p. 291.

8. *Ibid.,* pp. 298–299.

9. *Ibid.,* Vol. i, p. 315. From an extract taken from Edward D. Neill, *Virginia Velusta.*

10. "The World Encompassed by Sir Francis Drake," *Old South Leaflets,* Vol. v, pp. 79, 321–322.

11. Alexander Brown, *The Genesis of the United States,* Vol. i, pp. 53–54.

12. *The Sermons of John Donne* (Berkeley, 1959), Vol. iv, pp. 274–275.

13. Alexander Young, *Chronicles of the First Planters* (Boston, 1846), p. 133.

14. *The Compact, Charter and Laws of the Colony of New Plymouth* (Boston, 1836), p. 17.

15. *The Founding of Massachusetts* (Massachusetts Historical Society, 1930), p. 45.
16. *Dignitis Dei, New Discoveries* (London, 1652, 1660). Letter of John Eliot is in the second edition.

### VII. CHALLENGE OF THE ALGONQUIAN LANGUAGE

1. "New England's First Fruits," *M. H. S. Coll.*, 1st series (1806), p. 246.
2. William Wallace Tooker, *John Eliot's First Indian Teacher and Interpreter, Cockenoe-de-Long Island* (New York, 1896), p. 12.
3. *Key to the Indian Language, Publications of the Narragansett Club,* 1st series (1866), Vol. I, p. 29.
4. *The Indian Grammar Begun, M. H. S. Coll.,* 2nd series (1832), p. 312.
5. *Ibid.,* p. 313.
6. *The Day-Breaking of the Gospel among the Indians of New-England, M. H. S. Coll.,* 3rd series (1834). This occasion is reported on p. 4.
7. *The Indian Bible,* 1663. Translation by William Biglow, *History of the Town of Natick* (Boston, 1830), pp. 48–50, from *Mithridates,* of Johann Christoph Adelung (Berlin, 1812).
8. End of *The Indian Grammar Begun, M. H. S. Coll.,* 2nd series (1832), Vol. IX, p. 312.

### VIII. AT WABAN'S WIGWAM

1. *The Day-Breaking, if not the Sun-Rising of the Gospel with the Indians in New England* (London, 1647), p. 9. John Winthrop has a word about these first meetings, *Journal,* Vol. II, pp. 303–305.
2. This request was immediately granted. *Records of the Colony of Massachusetts Bay in New England,* edited by Nathaniel Shurtleff (1854), Vol. III, p. 85; recording action of November 4, 1646, "for ye good of ye Indians." A commission was appointed to attend to this matter. John Eliot was a member of it.
3. *Day-Breaking,* p. 20. The next tract, *The Clear Sun-shine of the Gospel Breaking forth upon the Indians in New England,* lists a similar code of laws made by the Indians of Concord, 29 laws, pp. 39–40.
4. Indian prayers are in *The Day-Breaking,* p. 21.

### IX. THE SOCIETY FOR
### THE PROPAGATION OF THE GOSPEL

1. John Winthrop's *Journal,* notes this meeting, Vol. II, pp. 308, 309.
2. Raymond Phineas Stearns, "The Weld-Peter Mission to England,"

*Publications of the Colonial Society of Massachusetts* (1933–1937), Vol. XXXII, pp. 188–246.

3. *op. cit.,* Vol. VII, p. 1, *supra.* Authorship of this tract is uncertain, but Thomas Shepard, who was present, is the probable author.
4. Thomas Shepard's name is on the title page of this tract.
5. Contains letters of John Eliot and Thomas Mayhew.
6. It was published in 1652 (1st ed.)
7. William Kellaway, *The New England Company* (New York, 1961), pp. 12–16, gives a summary statement of this bill. Mr. Kellaway's book-long treatment from the society's papers, is full and authoritative.
8. Richard Walden Hale, *Tercentenary History of the Roxbury Latin School* (Cambridge, 1946), pp. 33–37.
9. Quoted, Kellaway, p. 93. John Eliot's salary, at first £40, half from Lady Armin's legacy, was finally £50.
10. *The Works of Robert Boyle,* edited by Thomas Birch, Vol. I, pp. CCV–CCXIV, are letters of John Eliot to Boyle. The charter of the corporation is included in the Appendix, pp. CLIV–CLVIII.

### X. NATICK, FIRST OF THE PRAYING TOWNS

1. Oct. 8, 1650.
2. *Day-Breaking, op. cit., M. H. S. Coll.,* 3rd series, Vol. IV, p. 8.
3. *A Farther Discovery of the Present State of the Indians in New-England* (London, 1651), p. 138.
4. Exodus 18:17–26.
5. Quoted by William Biglow, *History of the Town of Natick, Massachusetts* (Boston, 1850), pp. 22–23.
6. *The Glorious Progress of the Gospel Amongst the Indians in New-England* (London, 1649), *M. H. S. Coll.,* 3rd series (1834), Vol. IV, p. 86.
7. *M. H. S. Coll.,* 3rd series, Vol. IV, p. 88.
8. *Strength Out of Weakness; or a Glorious Manifestation of the Further Progresse of the Gospel among the Indians in New-England, M. H. S. Coll.,* 3rd series (1834), pp. 189–191.
9. Caleb Cheeseaumuck, A. B. Harvard, 1665.

### XI. THE INDIAN BIBLE

1. In a letter to Edward Winslow, *A Farther Discovery, op. cit.,* pp. 121–122.
2. March 18, 1653, *Digitus Dei,* 1660 ed.

3. Gustavus S. Paine, *The Learned Men* (New York, 1959), p. 1.
4. To Thomas Thorowgood, *Digitus Dei,* 1660 ed.
5. Selected from various lists of questions in the *Tracts.*
6. A chapter in *The Memorial History of Boston,* by Justin Winsor, "The Indian Tongue and its Literature," Vol. I, pp. 405–480; another in *American Antiquarian Society Proceedings* (1873), pp. 14–43, with a list of "Books and Tracts in the Indian Language for the use of the Indians," pp. 45–62. This is a descriptive list of value.
7. April 21, 1664. Quoted by Pilling, *Bibliography of the Algonquian Language* (Washington, 1891), p. 141.

### XII. THE FIRST INDIAN CHURCH

1. *Tears of Repentance: or a further Narrative of the Progress of the Gospel amongst the Indians in New-England* (London, 1653), *M. H. S. Coll.,* 3rd series (1834), Vol. IV, pp. 227–260.
2. *Ibid.,* pp. 229–231.
3. *Ibid.,* pp. 231–232.
4. *Ibid.,* pp. 234–240.
5. *Ibid.,* pp. 248–249.
6. *Ibid.,* pp. 258–259.
7. *Ibid.,* pp. 245–246.
8. *Ibid.,* pp. 252–253.
9. *Ibid.,* p. 253.
10. *Ibid.,* pp. 242–243.
11. *A Late and Further Manifestation of the Progress of the Gospel amongst the Indians in New-England* (London, 1655), *M. H. S. Coll.* (1834), 3rd series, Vol. IV, pp. 277–284.
12. *A Further Accompt of the Progress of the Gospel,* 1659, Sabin Reprints.
13. *New England Historical and Genealogical Register* (1882), Vol. XXXVI, pp. 291–293.
14. *Ibid.,* Vol. XXXVI, p. 295.

### XIII. MORE PRAYING TOWNS

1. *Historical Collections of the Indians in New England, M. H. S. Coll.* (1806), Vol. I, pp. 144–226; Chapter VII, 180–196 describes the towns founded by John Eliot.
2. *Ibid.,* p. 184.
3. *Ibid.,* pp. 184–185.
4. *Ibid.,* pp. 185–186.
5. *Ibid.,* pp. 186–188.

6. *Ibid.,* p. 188.
7. *Ibid.,* pp. 188–189.
8. *Ibid.,* pp. 189–193.
9. Various letters from Thomas Mayhew are included in the *Tracts.* Other titles also came from his pen; Thomas Prince, *Mayhew's Indian Converts,* 1727, Appendix from Experience Mayhew, *Indian Narratives,* 1727.
10. From *Indian Converts,* Appendix.
11. *Historical Collections, op. cit.,* p. 195.

### XIV. THE PRAYING INDIANS IN KING PHILIP'S WAR

1. For a selected bibliography of King Philip's War, as well as an excellently detailed and accurate account of the years, 1675, 1676, see Douglas Edward Leach, *Flintlock and Tomahawk* (New York, 1958).
2. Leach, pp. 30–33.
3. John Eliot gives an account of a conversation with him in "The Glorious Progress," *M. H. S. Coll.,* 3rd series, Vol. IV, pp. 82–83. This farewell speech is variously translated. Samuel G. Drake, *Aboriginal Races of North America* (New York, 1888), p. 278.
4. *Records of the Colony of Massachusetts Bay,* Vol. V, pp. 57, 64.
5. *Roxbury Church Book,* Document 114, p. 193.
6. *Ibid.,* pp. 194–195.
7. *N. E. H. G. Register* (1852), Vol. VI, 297.
8. *Roxbury Church Record,* Document 114, p. 196.

### XV. A NEW START

1. *M. H. S. Proc.* (1879–1880), Vol. XVII, pp. 249–250. To Ashurst, December 1, 1671.
2. To Boyle, June 21, 1683.
3. To Boyle, November 27, 1683.
4. August 29, 1686.
5. August 29, 1686.
6. July 7, 1688.
7. Samuel Sewall had been treasurer of the Boston commissioners for many years.

# SELECTED BIBLIOGRAPHY

Adams, Nehemiah, *The Life of John Eliot*. Boston, 1847.

Battis, Henry, *Saints and Sectaries*. Williamsburg, 1962.

Baxter, Richard, *A Call to the Unconverted*. Glasgow, 1825.

Bayley, Lewis, *The Practice of Piety*. Edinburgh, 1792.

Bell, A. F. G., *Juan Ginés de Sepúlveda*. Hispanic Society of America, Notes and Monographs, Vol. IX, pp. 1–61.

Bethel, Samuel Leslie, *The Cultural Revolution of the Seventeenth Century*. London, 1951.

Biglow, William, *History of the Town of Natick, Massachusetts*. Boston, 1830.

Birch, Thomas, "Life of Robert Boyle," Vol. I, *The Works of Robert Boyle*. 6 vols. London, 1772.

Boyle, Robert, *The Works of Robert Boyle*, Thomas Birch, ed. London, 1772.

———, Letters of Robert Boyle, Vol. VI.

Browne, Alexander, *The Genesis of the United States*. Boston & New York, 1890.

Busk, H. W., *A Sketch of the Origin and Recent History of the New England Company*. London, 1884.

Byington, Ezra Hoyt, "John Eliot, the Puritan Missionary to the Indians," in *Papers of the American Society of Church History*. Vol. VIII, pp. 109–145. New York, 1897.

———, *The Puritan in England and New England*. Boston, 1896.

———, *The Puritan as a Colonist and Reformer*. Boston, 1899.

Chamberlain, David, *Eliot of Massachusetts*. London, 1928.

Clark, Thomas, *Historical Account of John Eliot, Massachusetts Historical Society Collections*, 1st series (1802), Vol. VIII, pp. 5–35.

Cornish, Louis C., "John Eliot," Extract from the *Proceedings of the Unitarian Historical Society*, Vol. VII, Pt. 1, July 10, 1941.

Costello, William T., *The Scholastic Curriculum at Early Seventeenth-Century Cambridge*. Harvard University Press, Cambridge, Mass., 1958.

Culver, John Blaine, *Theology of John Eliot, a Study in Puritan Adaptation*. Graduate College, University of Illinois (Unpublished).

De Normandie, James, *Address on the Apostle Eliot*, Mar. 17, 1907.

——, *An Historical Sketch of the First Church in Roxbury*, 1896.

——, "John Eliot, the Apostle to the Indians," *Harvard Theological Review*, July, 1912, pp. 249–370.

Dexter, Henry M., "Early Missionary Labors among the Indians of the Massachusetts Colony," *The Sabbath at Home*, 1898, pp. 272, 332, 385, 461.

Dillaway, Charles Knapp, *A History of the Grammar School at Roxbury*, Roxbury, 1860.

Donne, John, *An Anatomy of the World* (a facsimile of the first edition). Roxburghe Club, Cambridge, 1951.

Drake, Samuel G., *The Old Indian Chronicle*. Boston, 1867.

——, "Roxbury in the Colonial Period," Winsor's *Memorial History of Boston*. Vol. I, pp. 401–422. Boston, 1881.

——, *The Town of Roxbury*. Roxbury, 1878.

——, *Records Relating to the Early History of Boston*. (Roxbury), Vol. xxxiv.

Du Ponceau, Peter S., "Notes and Observations on Eliot's Indian Grammar, addressed to John Pickering, Esq." *M. H. S. Coll.* (1832), 2nd series, Vol. ix, after p. 313.

Eames, Wilberforce, *Bibliographical Notes on Eliot's Indian Bible*. Washington, D. C., 1895.

——, *John Eliot and the Indians*, Being Letters addressed to Jonathan Hammer of Barnstaple, England. Reproduced from original MSS. in possession of Theodore N. Vail. New York, 1915.

Ellis, Arthur B., *History of the First Church in Boston, 1630–1880*. Boston, 1881.

Ellis, Charles M., *The History of Roxbury Town*. Boston, 1847.

Ellis, George Edward, "The Indians of Eastern Massachusetts," Winsor's *Memorial History of Boston*, Vol. I, pp. 241–274. Boston, 1881.

——, "Las Casas and the Relations of the Spaniards to the Indians," Winsor's *Memorial History of Boston*, Vol. ii, pp. 299–348.

Evans, Pritchard, *Theories of Primitive Religion*. Oxford, 1965.

Essex County, England, *Publications of the Record Office*. Chelmsford, England.

Ford, John W., *Some Correspondence between the Governors and Treasurers of the New England Company*, 1657–1714. London, 1896.

*The Founding of Massachusetts*, M. H. S. Boston, 1930, p. 45.

Francis, Convers, *Life of John Eliot, the Apostle to the Indians*. Boston, 1896.

Gookin, Daniel, *An Historical Account of the Doings and Sufferings of the Christian Indians* in the Years, 1675, 1676, 1677, *American Antiquarian Society Collections and Transactions*. Essex, 1836.

Gookin, Daniel, "History of the Christian Indians," *A. A. S.*, Vol. II, *Archeologia Americana*, 1896, pp. 433–634.

——, "Historical Collections of the Indians in New England," (1806), *M. H. S. Coll.*, Vol. I, pp. 141–226.

Gookin, Frederick William, *Daniel Gookin*. Chicago, 1912.

Gray, Arthur, *Jesus College*. University of Cambridge, College Series, London, 1902.

Hale, Richard Walden, *Tercentenary History of the Roxbury Latin School*. Cambridge, 1946.

Hanke, Lewis, *Aristotle and the American Indians*. Chicago, 1959.

——, *The First Social Experiments in America*. Cambridge (Harvard), 1935.

Haraszti, Zoltan, *The Bay Psalm Book*, 1640; facsimile, 1956.

——, *The Enigma of the Bay Psalm Book*. Chicago, 1956.

Haven, S. F., "Books and Tracts in the Indian Language," *American Antiquarian Society Proceedings*, Oct. 1873.

Henson, Herbert Hensley, *Studies in English Religion in the Seventeenth Century*. New York, 1903.

Higginson, John, *New England's Plantation*. London, 1630.

Hill, Christopher, *Society and Puritanism in Pre-Revolutionary England*. London, 1964.

*The Historical Account of John Eliot, M. H. S. Coll.* (1802) 1st series, Vol. VIII.

Homer, Jonathan, "Description and History of Newton, in the County of Middlesex," *M. H. S. Coll.*, 1st series, Vol. V, pp. 253–280.

Hurd, D. Hamilton, *History of Middlesex County*. Vol. I, Chapter XXXVI. Philadelphia, 1890.

Hutchinson, Thomas, *The History of the Colony and Province of Massachusetts Bay*, Lawrence S. Mayo, ed., 3 vols., Cambridge, 1936.

The Indian Bible, *Mamusse Wunneetupanatamwe Up-Biblum God*, 1663 and 1685 editions, Cambridge.

*Inventory of the Historic Monuments of Hertfordshire*, Royal Commission, 1911.

*John Rylands Library Bulletin*, Vol. V (1918–1920), pp. 102–110; Vol. XV, pp. 138–176; pp. 442–466.

Kellaway, William, *The New England Company, 1649–1776*. New York, 1961.

Kenway, Albert Cliften, *Memorials of Old Essex*. London, 1908.

Leach, Douglas Edward, *Flintlock and Tomahawk, New England in King Philip's War*. New York, 1958.

Lechford, Thomas, *Plain Dealing or News from New England*. 1867.

"A Letter about the Present State of Christianity among the Christianized Indians," 1705.

MacNutt, Francis Augustus, *Bartholomew De Las Casas His Life, His Apostulate, and his Writings.* New York and London, 1909.

Mather, Cotton, *Magnalia Christi Americana,* Or, the Ecclesiastical History of New England, 2 vols., Hartford, 1820, containing "The Triumphs of the Reformed Religion in America" and "The Life of the Renowned John Eliot."

Mayhew, Experience, *Indian Converts.* 1727.

——, *Indian Narratives.* Boston, 1727.

——, "Experience Mayhew's Letters on Indian Language," *New England Historical and Genealogical Register* (1885), Vol. 39.

Morison, Samuel Eliot, "John Eliot," *Builders of the Bay Colony.* Boston and New York, 1930.

——, *Christopher Columbus, Mariner.* Boston, 1942, 1955.

——, *The Founding of Harvard College.* Cambridge, 1935.

——, "Precedence at Harvard College," *A. A. S. Proc.,* 1933, pp. 371–431.

Morris, Richard B., *Fair Trial.* New York, 1952.

Mullinger, James Bass, *Cambridge Characteristics.* London, 1867;

——, *The University of Cambridge.* Cambridge, 1873.

Neal, Daniel, *The History of New England.* London, 1747.

Norbeck, Edward, *Religion in Primitive Society.* New York, 1961.

Norden, John, *A Progress of Piety,* 1591, 1596; Parker Reprint, Cambridge, 1847.

Notestein, Wallace, *The English People on the Eve of Colonization.* New York, 1954.

Orme, Rev. William, *The Life and Times of Richard Baxter.* London, 1830.

Paine, Gustavus, *The Learned Men.* New York, 1959.

Parks, George Bruner, *Richard Hakluyt and the English Voyages, American Geographical Society.* New York, 1928.

Pickering, John, "The Massachusetts Language," *M. H. S. Coll.,* (1832), Vol. ix, pp. 233–242.

Pilling, James C., *"Bibliography of the Algonquian Language,* U.S. Bureau of Ethnology. Washington, 1891.

Porter, H. C., *Reformation and Reaction in Tudor Cambridge.* Cambridge, 1958.

Powicke, F. G., "Some Unpublished Correspondence of the Reverend Richard Baxter and the Reverend John Eliot, 1656–1682," *Bulletin of the John Rylands Library,* Vol. v, 1915; Vol. xv, 1931. Manchester, England, 1931.

Purchas, Samuel, *Hakluytus Posthumus,* or *Purchas His Pilgrimes,* Vol. xviii. Glasgow, 1906.

Radin, Paul, *Primitive Religion, Its Nature and Origin.* London, 1938.

——, *The World of Primitive Man.* New York, 1953.

Rogers, Richard, and Ward, Samuel, *Two Elizabethan Puritan Diaries*. Chicago, 1933.

*Roxbury Land and Church Records*, City Document No. 114. Boston, 1881.

Shepard, Thomas, *The Sincere Convert*. London, 1641.

Shurtleff, Nathaniel B., *Records of the Governor and Company of the Massachusetts Bay in New England*, Vols. I–IV. Boston, 1854.

Standing, Percy Cross, *Memorials of Old Hertfordshire*. London, 1915.

Stearns, Raymond Phineas, "The Weld-Peter Mission to England," *Colonial Society Transactions*, Vol. XXXII, 1934, pp. 188–246.

Sterry-Cooper, William, *Edward Winslow*. Birmingham, England, 1953.

Stiles, Ezra, "Anne Hutchinson's Church Trial," *M. H. S. Proc.* (1888–89), Presented by Franklin B. Dexter, pp. 159–191.

*The Tercentenary Celebration of the First Church in Roxbury, 1630–1930*.

Thomas, Isaiah, *The History of Printing in America*. Albany, New York, 1814.

Thorowgood, Thomas, *Digitus Dei: New Discoveries*. London, 1652.

Thwing, Walter Eliot, *History of the First Church in Roxbury*. Boston, 1908.

Tooker, William Wallace, *John Eliot's First Indian Teacher and Interpreter*. New York, 1896.

Trumbull, J. Hammond, "The Indian Tongue and its Literature as Fashioned by Eliot and Others," Winsor's *Memorial History of Boston*, Vol. I, pp. 465–480.

———, *Origin and Early Progress of Indian Missions in New England*. Worcester, 1874. Also entitled "Report of the Council," *Amer. Ant. Soc. Proc.*, 1872–1875, pp. 14–43.

Vaughan, Alden T., *New England Frontier, Puritans and Indians, 1620–1675*. Boston, 1965.

Venn, J. & J.A., *Alumni Cantabrigienses*, Cambridge, 1922. Part I, Vol. II.

Venning, William Marshall, "Origin of the New England Company," *Transactions of the Royal Historical Society*, Vol. II, pp. 293–301. London, 1885.

*The Victoria History of the County of Essex*, Vols. III–V. London, 1903–66.

*Vital Records of Roxbury*, Vol. I, Births; Vol. II, Marriages and Deaths. Salem, Mass. 1925.

Waters, Henry F., *Genealogical Gleanings in England*. Boston, 1901.

Watson, Foster, *The English Grammar Schools to 1660*. Cambridge, 1908.

Weis, Frederick L., "The New England Company of 1649 and its Missionary Enterprises," *Col. Soc. Trans.*, Vol. XXXVIII, 1947–1951.

Welde, Thomas, *A Short Story of the Rise, reign and ruin of the Antinomians.* London, 1644.

White, Helen C., *The Tudor Books of Devotion.* Univ. of Wisconsin, 1951.

Willis, Robert, *The Architectural History of the University of Cambridge.* Cambridge, 1886.

Winship, George P., "Cost of Printing the first Indian Tracts," *Trans. of Col. Soc. of Mass.,* 1927, Vol. XXVI, pp. 85–86.

———, The First American Bible (a leaf). Boston, 1929.

———, "The New England Company of 1649 and John Eliot," *Prince Society,* 1920. *The Cambridge Press.* Philadelphia, 1945.

Winsor, Justin, *Memorial History of Boston.* Vols. I–IV. Boston, 1881.

———, "The New England Indians," *M. H. S. Proc.,* 2nd series, Vol. x, pp. 327–359.

Winters, William, "The Eliot Family," *N. E. H. G. Society* (1885), Vol. XXXIX, pp. 365–371.

———, "Notices of the Pilgrim Fathers, John Eliot and His Friends," *Transactions of the Royal Society* (1882), Vol. x, pp. 267–311.

Winthrop, John, *The History of New England from 1630 to 1649.* Boston, 1825.

Wright, L. B., *Religion and Empire.* Chapel Hill, N.C., University of North Carolina Press, 1943.

Young, Alexander, *Chronicles of the First Planters.* Boston, 1846.

# INDEX